THE BEST OF BROCHURE DESIGN

#2386092

THE BEST OF BROCHURE DESIGN

Art Director
STEPHEN BRIDGES

Design and Production
SARA DAY

Production Manager
BARBARA STATES

Editor
JOSEPH FATTON

Typesetting
THE IMAGESETTER, INC.

Copyright © 1992 by Rockport Publishers, Inc.

First published in the United States of America by:
Rockport Publishers, Inc.
P.O. Box 396
Five Smith Street
Rockport, Massachusetts 01966
Telephone: (508) 546-9590
Fax: (508) 546-7141
Telex: 5106019284 ROCKORT PUB

Distributed to the book trade and art trade in the U.S.
and Canada by:
North Light, an imprint of
F & W Publications
1507 Dana Avenue
Cincinnati, Ohio 45207
Telephone: (513) 531-2222

Other Distribution by:
Rockport Publishers, Inc.
Rockport, Massachusetts 01966

ISBN 1-56496-004-8

3 5 7 9 10 8 6 4

Printed in Singapore

THE BEST OF BROCHURE DESIGN

ROCKPORT
PUBLISHERS

DISTRIBUTED BY
NORTH LIGHT BOOKS
CINCINNATI, OHIO

CONTENTS

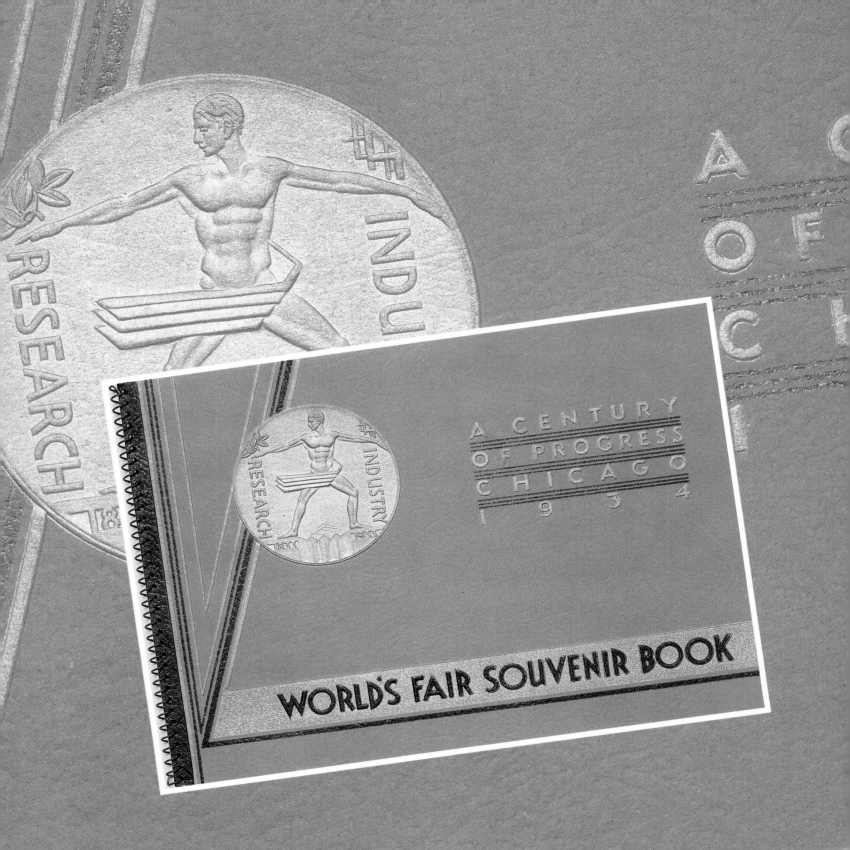

A CENTURY
OF PROGRESS
CHICAGO
1 9 3 4

WORLD'S FAIR SOUVENIR BOOK

INTRODUCTION

"Why don't you send me one of your brochures?" I say to the telephone solicitor whose product I have no interest in. When the brochure arrives, it misses its opportunity to impress me, so I toss it into the trash.

Brochures, by their nature, are ephemeral. Why, then, do we find antiques stores filled with so many booklets, maps, guides, and - yes - brochures?

One of my most treasured possessions is a souvenir booklet from the 1933-34 Chicago World's Fair. The cover is a colorful and exquisite example of art deco design. The booklet's typography, colors, and graphics reflect an era that ended long ago.

Some publications, even those originally designed for an immediate, short-lived purpose, remain vital and interesting today. They succeeded when they were originally produced, and they still communicate their message to the reader. Today's effective brochures - if they survive the "trash toss" - may also captivate and interest readers of tomorrow.

Most designers don't set out to produce a brochure with the idea of selling it at an antiques store. They want to sell a product, promote an event, or convey an idea. A compelling and effective brochure, however, will still be around decades after its original purpose has been served.

This book is a collection of wonderful, innovative brochures that advertise a particular product or promote a particular event. The range of design techniques displayed is impressive. There are pop-ups, fold-outs, pull-tabs,, and novelty mailers. There are two-color projects and some that required several passes through a multicolor press. Some fit in a #10 envelope, and some are more than 2 feet long.

That they were effective in selling or promoting makes these brochures successful in their own right. But they also have the chance to succeed in another way: by passing the test of time.

Sheree Clark
Clark is director of client services and a principal at Sayles Graphic Design in Des Moines, Iowa.

INSTITUTIONAL

1
Design Firm, **Sayles Graphic Design**
Art Director, **John Sayles**
Designer, **John Sayles**
Illustrator, **John Sayles**
Copywriter, **Wendy Lyons**
Client, **Open Bible Churches**
Four colors on James River Tuscan

Mailed in a corrugated box, this promotion for a national youth convention features an unusually shaped brochure and postcards.

2
Design Firm, **Sayles Graphic Design**
Art Director, **John Sayles**
Designer, **John Sayles**
Illustrator, **John Sayles**
Copywriter, **Carol Mouchka**
Client, **Dowling High School**
Three colors on King James

A custom die-cut allows this brochure to become its own envelope. The "Chart Your Course" theme was underscored with a compass glued to the last panel in the mailing.

1
Design Firm, **Sayles Graphic Design**
Art Director, **John Sayles**
Designer, **John Sayles**
Illustrator, **John Sayles**
Copywriter, **Wendy Lyons**
Client, **Central Life Assurance**
Four colors on James River Graphika Parchment

*Because a limited number of brochures were required,
this project was silk-screened. The spiral-bound piece
features a corrugated cover and is mailed in a box-
like envelope.*

1
Design Firm, **John Sayles**
Art Director, **John Sayles**
Designer, **John Sayles**
Illustrator, **John Sayles**
Copywriter, **Julie Sommerlot**
Client, **University of California, Santa Barbara**
Three colors on James River Tuscan Terra

*This self-mailing brochure has a dual purpose: when
unfolded, it becomes a full-size poster.*

1
Design Firm, **Sayles Graphic Design**
Art Director, **John Sayles**
Designer, **John Sayles**
Illustrator, **John Sayles**
Copywriter, **Wendy Lyons**
Client, **University of California, Berkeley**
Four colors on Neenah Classic Crest; Neenah Millstone

The illustration in this brochure spans over 8 1/2 feet in length and took more than 120 hours to complete.

1
Design Firm, **Sayles Graphic Design**
Art Director, **John Sayles**
Designer, **John Sayles**
Illustrator, **John Sayles**
Copywriter, **Wendy Lyons**
Client, **University of California,
Berkeley**
Three colors on James River Tuscan Terra

*The cover of this brochure is silk-screened
on corrugated cardboard. The inside is
offset-printed on fine paper and saddle-
stitched into the cover with 2 inch
industrial staples.*

2
Design Firm, **Sayles Graphic Design**
Art Director, **John Sayles**
Designer, **John Sayles**
Illustrator, **John Sayles**
Copywriter, **Wendy Lyons**
Client, **Central Life Assurance**
Three colors on chipboard

*This brochure is silk-screened onto
chipboard for a rustic look. The "envelope"
is a silk-screened corrugated cardboard
box.*

1
Design Firm, **Sayles Graphic Design**
Art Director, **John Sayles**
Designer, **John Sayles**
Photographer, **Bill Nellans**
Copywriter, **Mary Langen-Goldstien**
Client, **Buena Vista College**
Four colors on James River

Sent in a clear plastic tube, this mailer's "point of view" theme is revealed by a custom kaleidoscope with the Buena Vista logo inside.

2
Design Firm, **Sayles Graphic Design**
Art Director, **John Sayles**
Designer, **John Sayles**
Illustrator, **John Sayles**
Photographer, **Bill Nellans**
Copywriter, **Wendy Lyons**
Client, **Buena Vista College**
Four colors on James River

The paper used for this project is specially made by the James River paper mill. John Sayles developed the paper color with mill representatives and was able to specify the finish, color of flocking, etc.

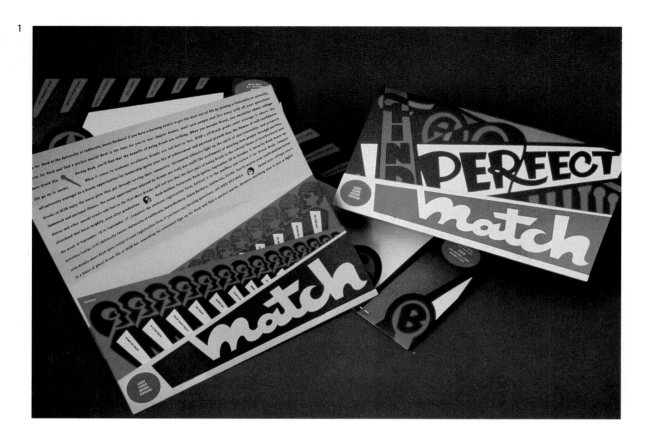

1
Design Firm, **Sayles Graphic Design**
Art Director, **John Sayles**
Designer, **John Sayles**
Illustrator, **John Sayles**
Copywriter, **Wendy Lyons**
Client, **University of California,
Santa Barbara**
Four colors on James River

*The brochure opens to reveal matchsticks
with human features.*

2
Design Firm, **Sayles Graphic Design**
Art Director, **John Sayles**
Designer, **John Sayles**
Illustrator, **John Sayles**
Copywriter, **LeAnn Koerner**
Client, **University of California,
Santa Barbara**
Four colors on plastic corrugated

*This oversized postcard is silk-screened
onto a plastic, translucent corrugated
material. For opaque areas, a block of
inked areas is planned into the design.*

1
Design Firm, **Sayles Graphic Design**
Art Director, **John Sayles**
Designer, **John Sayles/Keith Sandvig**
Illustrator, **John Sayles**
Photographer, **Stock photos**
Client, **Alexander Hamilton Life**
Eight colors on Neenah Classic Crest

*The individual pop-ups in this brochure require
hand-gluing.*

1
Design Firm, **Sayles Graphic Design**
Art Director, **John Sayles**
Designer, **John Sayles**
Illustrator, **John Sayles**
Copywriter, **Sheree Clark**
Client, **Western Regional
Greek Conference**
Two colors on Cougar

With a radio theme as its base, this brochure features music-inspired illustrations, in a perfect-bound format.

2
Design Firm, **Sayles Graphic Design**
Art Director, **John Sayles**
Designer, **John Sayles**
Illustrator, **John Sayles**
Copywriter, **Mary Langen-Goldstien**
Client, **Loyola University, Chicago**
Two colors on Gilbert Oxford

Text-weight paper is adhered to corrugated cardboard after printing to create the box and "license plates." A map inside unfolds to become a folder.

1
Design Firm, **Sayles Graphic Design**
Art Director, **John Sayles**
Designer, **John Sayles**
Illustrator, **John Sayles**
Copywriter, **Wendy Lyons**
Client, **Drake University**
Five colors on Springhill

The mailer/brochure in this campaign includes a cassette recording and lyric sheet of the title song "We've Got the Beat."

2
Design Firm, **Sayles Graphic Design**
Art Director, **John Sayles**
Designer, **John Sayles**
Illustrator, **John Sayles**
Copywriter, **Wendy Lyons**
Client, **Western Regional Greek Conference**
Two colors on Cougar Natural

The "Hot Ideas" theme for this conference is reinforced by illustrations with such titles as "Now is the Time to Try a Hot Idea," "Hot Ideas are Sometimes Shocking," etc.

1
Design Firm, **Sayles Graphic Design**
Art Director, **John Sayles**
Designer, **John Sayles**
Copywriter, **Victor Boutrous**
Client, **Drake University**
Three colors and foil on Speckletone

2
Design Firm, **The Weller Institute for the Cure of Design, Inc.**
Art Director, **Don Weller**
Designer, **Don Weller**
Illustrator, **Don Weller**
Photographer, **Don Weller**
Copywriter, **Shel Weinstein**
Client, **Jewish Big Brothers**
Four colors

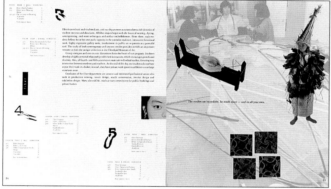

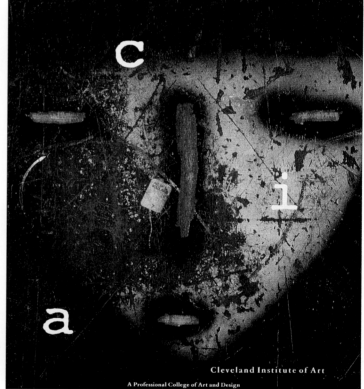

1
Design Firm, **Nesnadny & Schwartz**
Art Director, **Joyce Nesnadny/Ruth D'Emilia**
Designer, **Joyce Nesnadny/Ruth D'Emilia**
Photographer, **Nesnadny & Schwartz**
Copywriter, **Cleveland Institute of Art**
Client, **Cleveland Institute of Art**
Six colors on Warren Lustro

2
Design Firm, **Nesnadny & Schwartz**
Art Director, **Joyce Nesnadny/Ruth D'Emilia**
Designer, **Joyce Nesnadny/Ruth D'Emilia**
Copywriter, **Elizabeth Brown**
Client, **Cleveland Institute of Art**
Six colors on Mead Signature

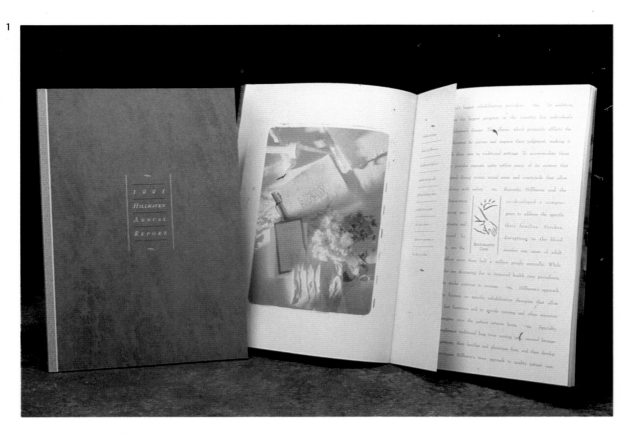

1
Design Firm, **Hornall Anderson Design Works**
Art Director, **Jack Anderson**
Designer, **Jack Anderson/Mary Hermes**
Illustrator, **Georgia Deaver**
Photographer, **Darrell Peterson**
Copywriter, **Tim Carroll**
Client, **Hillhaven Corp.**
Six colors on Sundance Felt cover, Starwhite
Vicksburg text

2
Design Firm, **Hornall Anderson Design Works**
Art Director, **Jack Anderson**
Designer, **Jack Anderson/Brian O'Neill/Lian Ng**
Illustrator, **John Fretz**
Copywriter, **Dr. Clem Pellet**
Client, **The Center for Oral and
Maxillofacial Surgery**

1
Design Firm, **Hornall Anderson Design Works**
Art Director, **Jack Anderson**
Designer, **Jack Anderson/Mary Hermes/**
Michelle Rieb
Illustrator, **Jonathan Combs**
Photographer, **Rosanne Olson**
Copywriter, **Tim Carroll**
Client, **Hillhaven Corp.**
Six colors on Passport Gypsum cover, Sterling
Litho Satin text

1
Design Firm, **Hornall Anderson Design Works**
Art Director, **Jack Anderson**
Designer, **Jack Anderson/Julie Tanagi-Lock/**
David Bates
Illustrator, **Jonathan Combs**
Photographer, **Tom Collicott**
Copywriter, **Nancy Adrian/Lori Jarman**
Client, **West One Bancorp**
Four process colors/three PMS colors (cover); four
process colors/one PMS on Quintessence dull
(narrative); two colors on Speckletone French (financials)

KANSAS CITY ART INSTITUTE

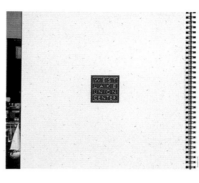

2

1
Design Firm, **Hornall Anderson Design Works**
Art Director, **Jack Anderson**
Designer, **Jack Anderson/Paula Cox**
Copywriter, **Fisher Properties**
Client, **Fisher Properties**
4 colors on Vintage, Wyndstone, Genesis

2
Design Firm, **Muller & Co.**
Art Director, **John Muller**
Designer, **Jane Weeks**
Copywriter, **John Krueger**
Client, **Kansas City Art Institute**
Six colors on LOE

1
Design Firm, **Muller & Co.**
Art Director, **John Muller/Jane Weeks/Mark Anderson/Patrice Eilts/Scott Chapman/Rich Kobs/Peter Corcoran**
Copywriter, **David Marks/Judy Spaar**
Client, **Kansas City Ad Club**
Two colors on Ikonofix dull

This brochure features 200-line screen duotones with dull semi-opaque inks.

1

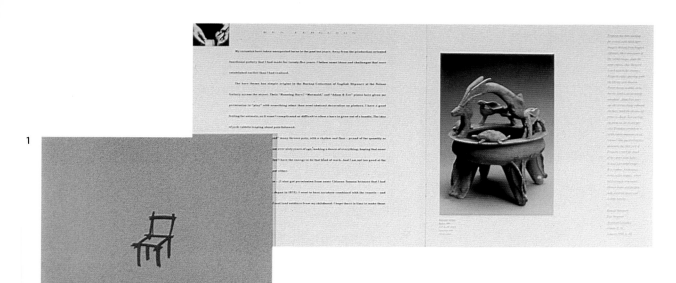

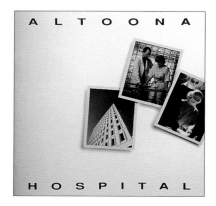

2

1
Design Firm, **Muller & Co.**
Art Director, **Jane Weeks/John Muller**
Designer, **Jane Weeks**
Client, **Kansas City Art Institute**
Three process colors/four PMS colors on Evergreen
Recycled 80-lb. cover, Karma 80-lb. text

2
Design Firm, **Gray Baumgarten Layport**
Art Director, **Vann Jennings**
Designer, **Vann Jennings**
Photographer, **Tom Gigliotti**
Copywriter, **Geoff Tolley**
Client, **Altoona Hospital**
Six colors

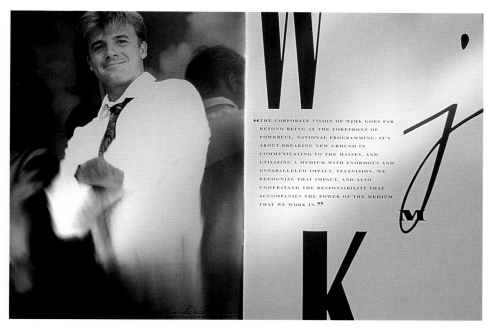

1
Design Firm, **Pinkhaus Design Corp.**
Art Director, **Tom Sterling**
Designer, **Tom Sterling**
Photographer, **Gallen Mei**
Copywriter, **Mark Keilar**
Client, **WJMK**
Six colors on Consolidated Reflections

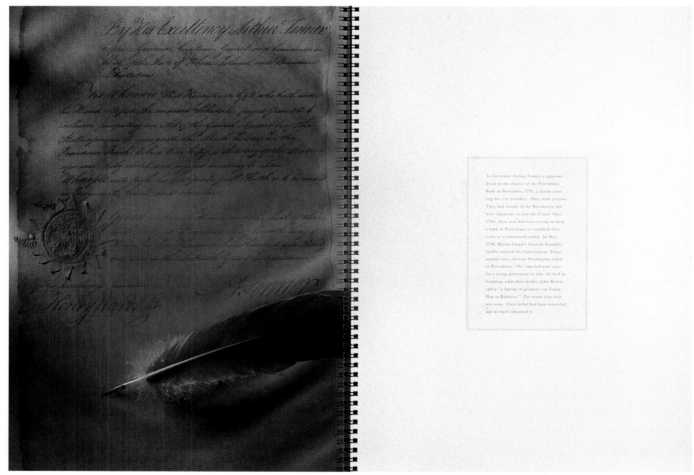

1
Design Firm, **Tyler Smith**
Art Director, **Tyler Smith**
Designer, **Tyler Smith**
Photographer, **Myron**
Copywriter, **History Factory**
Client, **Fleet National Bank**
Five colors on Warren

*This bank's 200th anniversary brochure visualizes
various tales relating to people and events in
Fleet's history.*

1
Design Firm, **Walcott-Ayers & Shore**
Creative Director, **Jim Walcott-Ayers**
Designer, **Elizabeth Pollina**
Illustrator, **Elizabeth Pollina**
Photographer, **Jim Walcott-Ayers**
Copywriter, **Jim Walcott-Ayers**
Client, **Saintsbury**
Six colors on Karma Natural 100-lb. book

Saintsbury is a winery client who wanted its story told without photos of "vineyards" or "barrels." The entire piece is computer-generated using Photoshop, Illustrator, and Quark.

2
Design Firm, **Sackett Design**
Art Director, **Mark Sackett**
Designer, **Mark Sackett**
Illustrator, **Walter Swarthout**
Copywriter, **Parc 55 Hotel**
Client, **Parc 55 Hotel**
Six colors on 80-lb. Quintessence gloss cover

1
Design Firm, **The Kuester Group**
Art Director, **Kevin B. Kuester**
Designer, **Bob Goebel**
Illustrator, **Bob Goebel**
Copywriter, **David Forney**
Client, **Trident Enterprises International, Inc.**
Four process colors/two match colors/one gloss/
one dull varnish on Potlatch Karma Natural 80-lb.
cover and Eloquence 85-lb. cover

1
Design Firm, **The Kuester Group**
Art Director, **Kevin B. Kuester, Brent Marmo**
Designer, **Bob Goebel, Brent Marmo**
Illustrator, **Geoffrey Moss**
Photographer, **James Williams**
Copywriter, **David Forney**
Client, **Potlatch Corp., Northwest Paper Division**
Four process colors/three match colors/one gloss
varnish on Potlatch Eloquence 100-lb. cover, 110-
lb. text, and Vintage Velvet Creme 100-lb. text

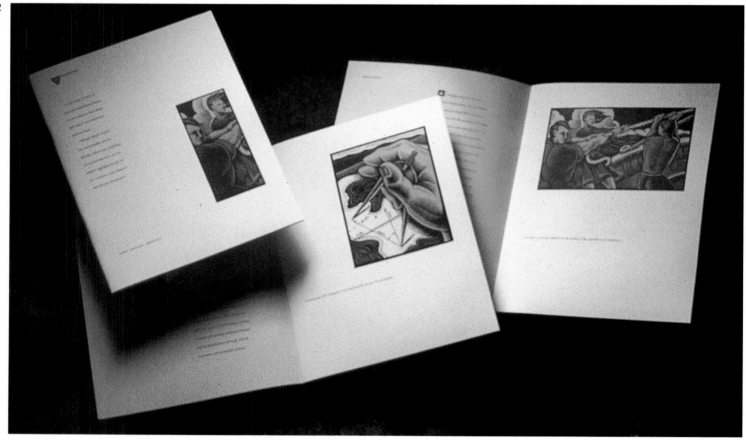

1
Design Firm, **The Kuester Group**
Art Director, **Kevin B. Kuester**
Designer, **Tim Sauer**
Illustrator, **Design Guys**
Photographer, **Jim Sims**
Copywriter, **Andrew Blankenburg (General Mills)**
Client, **General Mills, Inc.**
Eight colors on Potlatch Eloquence

2
Design Firm, **The Kuester Group**
Art Director, **Kevin B. Kuester**
Designer, **Tim Sauer**
Illustrator, **Design Guys**
Photographer, **Jim Schneff**
Copywriter, **Norstan, Inc.**
Client, **Norstan, Inc.**
Six colors and cover embossing on Potlatch
Vintage Velvet

1
Design Firm, **Allen Moore and Associates**
Art Director, **Allen Moore/Charles Melcher**
Designer, **Allen Moore**
Photographer, **John Rae**
Copywriter, **Heather McCuthen**
Client, **Dartmouth College Admissions**
Six colors on Centura Dull and Mohawk Superfine

1
Design Firm, **Stylism**
Art Director, **Dean Morris**
Designer, **Dean Morris**
Photographer, **Jose Pelaez**
Copywriter, **Skip Ohle/Carol Rubiano/**
Dean Morris
Client, **The Brooklyn Hospital Center**
Four colors on Mohawk Superfine

Each spread of this brochure describes the new
symbol's three shapes from a particular point of view
of the hospital organization.

Design Firm, **Chermayeff & Geismar, Inc.**
Design Director, **Steff Geissbuhler**
Designer, **Bill Anton**
Copywriter, **Alice Ozaroff**
Client, **Doral Hotels & Resorts**
Four colors on Karma

Design Firm, **Davies Associates**
Art Director, **Noel Davies**
Designer, **Cathy Tetef-Davies/Meredith Kamm**
Client, **R & T Development**
Eight colors on Teton cover and Reflections text

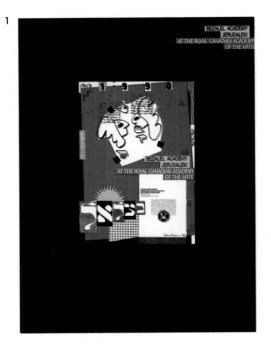

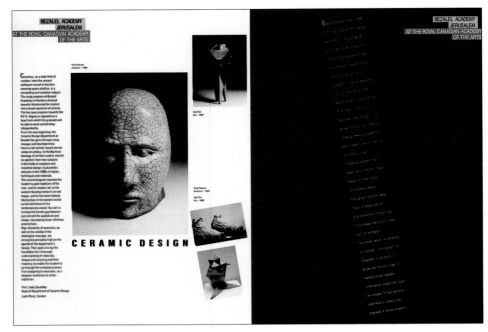

1
Design Firm, **Vardimon Design**
Art Director, **Yarom Vardimon**
Designer, **Yarom Vardimon**
Illustrator, **Yarom Vardimon**
Client, **Bezalel Academy Jerusalem**
Five colors

*The cover illustration for this brochure is reduced
from a full-sized poster for the exhibition.*

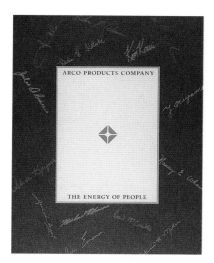

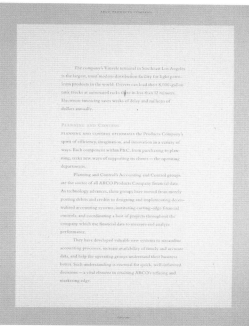

CENTER OF STYLE

1
Design Firm, **Besser Joseph Partners**
Art Director, **Rik Besser/Douglas Joseph**
Designer, **Rik Besser**
Photographer, **Eric Myer**
Copywriter, **Arco**
Client, **Arco**
Six colors on Vintage/Speckletone

2
Design Firm, **Communication Arts, Inc.**
Art Director, **Richard Foy**
Designer, **T. Keith Harley**
Photographer, **Dave Tejada/Stock**
Client, **Birtcher Kraus Properties**
Six colors on Speckletone cover, Low Cream dull

Conceived in the Vineyard

Clos du Bois started here, in the vineyards of the Alexander Valley, growing premium winegrapes. Before there was a winery—there was a commitment to quality that started in this valley.

Vineyard manager Steve Smit lives with his family on the Clos du Bois ranch. With a large crew of vineyard workers, Steve keeps a watchful eye on many factors—vine canopy, soil condition, pest management, crop control—which result in the outstanding fruit that has won Clos du Bois wines such acclaim.

Clos du Bois' vineyards are amongst the most extensive in Alexander Valley.

Aged with Care in Oak

Barrel aging remains essential to the perfection of most premium wines. Time-tested fermentation technology, aging in fine oak barrels and extended lees contact create the rich, smooth, balanced wines of Clos du Bois.

Creation of fine barrel-fermented Chardonnay and Sauvignon Blanc, and proper aging of red wines require the meticulous attention of our winemaker, Margaret Davenport, to every barrel. The harmony of flavors she achieves for Clos du Bois' wines results from her own vision of perfection.

A Passion for Excellence

For 15 years, product quality and customer satisfaction have been our primary goals at Clos du Bois.

Our product line has three distinct, harmonious levels: the Classic Varietals, the Vineyard Designates and Winemaker's Reserves. We take pride in every one of our award-winning wines.

1
Design Firm, **Glenn Martinez & Associates**
Art Director, **Kathleen Nelson**
Designer, **Glenn Martinez**
Illustrator, **Steve Doty**
Photographer, **Thomas Heinser**
Copywriter, **Clos Du Bois**
Client, **Clos Du Bois Winery**
Four colors on 80-lb. cover

2
Design Firm, **Glenn Martinez & Associates**
Art Director, **Kathleen Nelson**
Designer, **Glenn Martinez**
Illustrator, **Steve Doty**
Photographer, **Thomas Heinser**
Copywriter, **Clos Du Bois**
Client, **Clos Du Bois**
Four process colors, one-color flyleaf, foil emboss/
varnish on 80-lb. white Productolith cover and 80-
lb. bianco white Filage cover

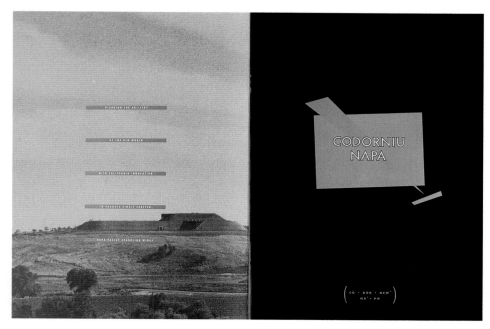

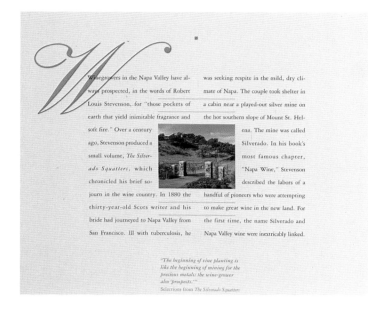

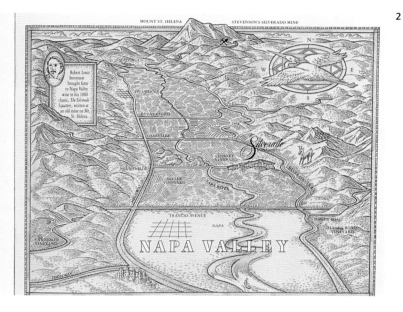

1
Design Firm, **Colonna, Farrell: Design Associates**
Art Director, **Ralph Colonna**
Designer, **Cynthia Maguire**
Photographer, **Doug Sterling**
Client, **Codorniu**
Four process colors/one metallic PMS color,
varnish on 100-lb. Centura gloss (cover) five PMS
colors and varnish (inside)

2
Design Firm, **Colonna, Farrell: Design Associates**
Art Director, **John Farrell**
Designer, **Cynthia Maguire**
Copywriter, **Jack Stuart**
Client, **Silverado Vineyards**
Four colors/one metallic PMS colors, spot varnish
and foil stamp on Gainsborough

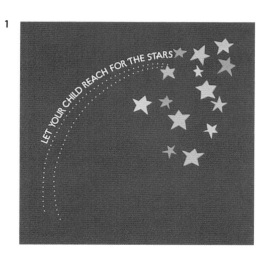

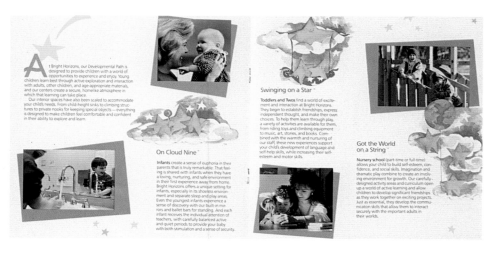

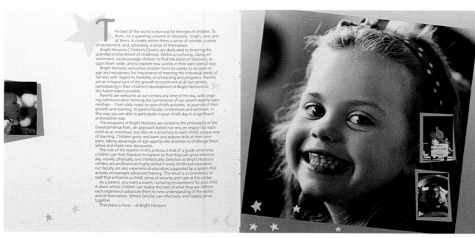

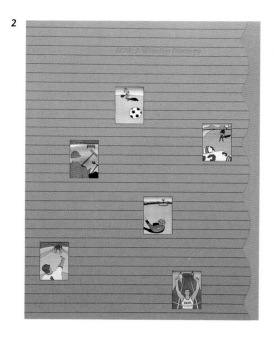

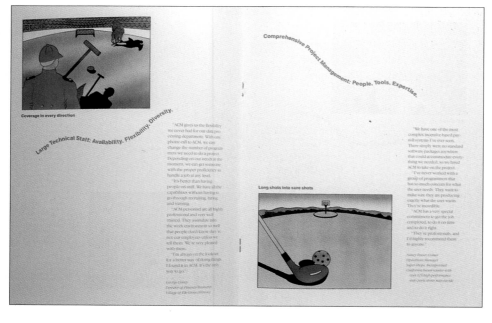

1
Design Firm, **Portfolio**
Art Director, **Wendy Terry/Busha Husak**
Designer, **Wendy Terry/Busha Husak**
Illustrator, **Ann Zeybekoglu**
Photographer, **Lenny Rubinstein**
Copywriter, **John Carroll**
Client, **Bright Horizons Day Care**
Two Toyo colors/two PMS colors on Becket RSVP
80-lb. (cover); four process colors and gray PMS
for duotones on Potlatch Karma 100-lb. (text)

*A star on the inside back cover flap is perfed so that a
child can punch it out and write his or her name and
hang it up or wear it.*

2
Design Firm, **Pangborn Design, Ltd.**
Art Director, **Dominic Pangborn**
Designer, **Ted Zablocki**
Illustrator, **Peter Schade**
Copywriter, **ACM Corp.**
Client, **ACM Corp.**
PMS 137 warm gray #5, aqueous coating, die-cut
folder, 100-lb. LOE gloss cover and 100-lb. LOE
gloss text

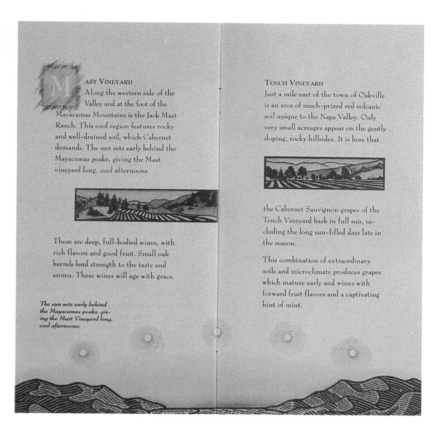

MAST VINEYARD
Along the western side of the Valley and at the foot of the Mayacamas Mountains is the Jack Mast Ranch. This cool region features rocky and well-drained soil, which Cabernet demands. The sun sets early behind the Mayacamas peaks. The sun sets early behind the Mast vineyard long, cool afternoons.

These are deep, full-bodied wines, with rich flavors and good fruit. Small oak barrels lend strength to the taste and aroma. These wines will age with grace.

The sun sets early behind the Mayacamas peaks, giving the Mast Vineyard long, cool afternoons.

TENCH VINEYARD
Just a mile east of the town of Oakville is an area of much-prized red volcanic soil unique to the Napa Valley. Only very small acreages appear on the gently sloping, rocky hillsides. It is here that

the Cabernet Sauvignon grapes of the Tench Vineyard bask in full sun, including the long sun-filled days late in the season.

This combination of extraordinary soils and microclimate produces grapes which mature early and wines with forward fruit flavors and a captivating hint of mint.

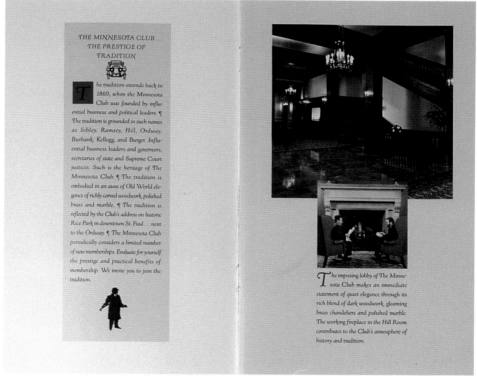

THE MINNESOTA CLUB... THE PRESTIGE OF TRADITION

The tradition extends back to 1869, when the Minnesota Club was founded by influential business and political leaders. The tradition is grounded in such names as Sibley, Ramsey, Hill, Ordway, Burbank, Kellogg, and Burger. Influential business leaders and governors, secretaries of state and Supreme Court justices. Such is the heritage of The Minnesota Club. The tradition is embodied in an aura of Old World elegance of richly carved woodwork, polished brass and marble. The tradition is reflected by the Club's address on historic Rice Park in downtown St. Paul... next to the Ordway. The Minnesota Club periodically considers a limited number of new memberships. Evaluate for yourself the prestige and practical benefits of membership. We invite you to join the tradition.

The imposing lobby of The Minnesota Club makes an immediate statement of quiet elegance through its rich blend of dark woodwork, gleaming brass chandeliers and polished marble. The working fireplace in the Hill Room contributes to the Club's atmosphere of history and tradition.

1
Design Firm, **Colonna, Farrell: Design Associates**
Art Director, **John Farrell/Tony Austin**
Designer, **Tony Austin**
Illustrator, **John Farrell/Mark Grey**
Client, **Gustave Niebaum**
Four process colors/two PMS colors on
Gainsborough Carma Natural

2
Design Firm, **Steve Lundgren Graphic Design**
Art Director, **Steve Lundgren**
Designer, **Steve Lundgren**
Photographer, **Kent DuFault/**
DuFault Photography
Copywriter, **Richard Cinquina**
Client, **The Minnesota Club**
Seven colors on Warren LOE dull Cream

*The black-and-white photos in this piece have been
color-separated and shifted to sepia-tone range.*

1

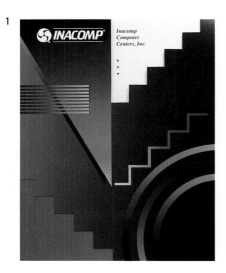

2

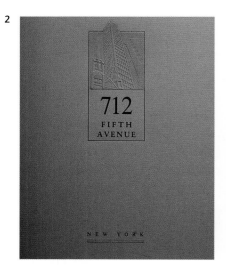

1
Design Firm, **Pangborn Design, Ltd.**
Art Director, **Dominic Pangborn**
Designer, **Dominic Pangborn/Ted Zablocki**
Illustrator, **Han-Eung Kim**
Copywriter, **Inacomp Computer Center, Inc.**
Client, **Inacomp Computer Center, Inc.**
Four process colors, special-mix red, dense black
and aqueous coating (one side), dense black and
PMS 423 on 100-lb. LOE gloss cover

2
Design Firm, **Pangborn Design, Ltd.**
Art Director, **Dominic Pangborn**
Designer, **Dominic Pangborn**
Photographer, **Robert Miller**
Copywriter, **The Taubman Co.**
Client, **The Taubman Co.**
Six color/match grays on Seamen Patrick Ikonolux,
bs. 111

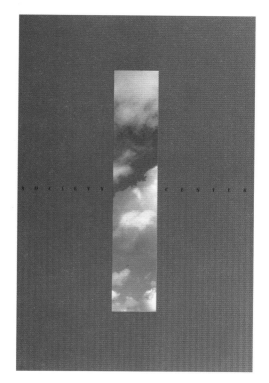

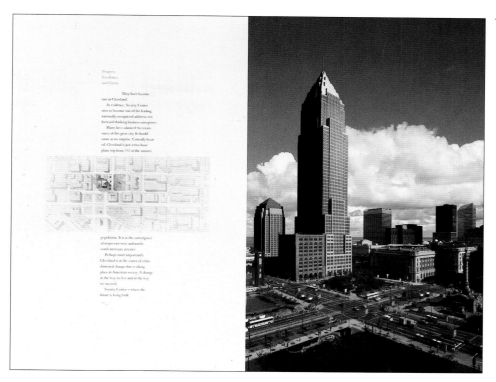

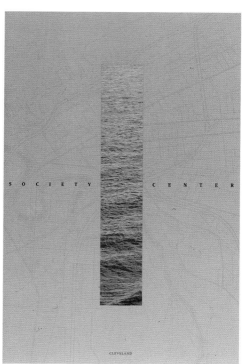

1
Design Firm, **Nesnadny & Schwartz**
Art Director, **Okey Nestor/Ruth D'Emilia/Mark Schwartz**
Designer, **Okey Nestor/Ruth D'Emilia**
Illustrator, **Lowell Williams**
Photographer, **Nesnadny & Schwartz**
Architectural Composite, **Hedrich Blessing**
Client, **Richard E. Jacobs/David H. Jacobs**
13 colors on Quintessence

1

 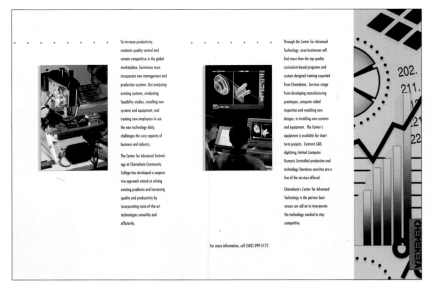

2

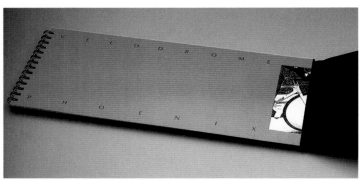 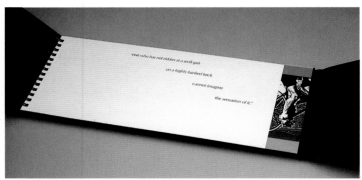

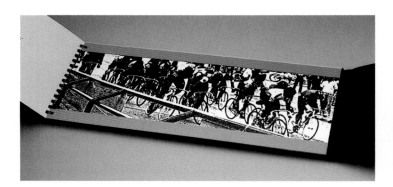 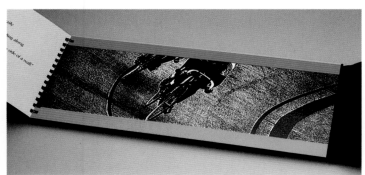

1
Design Firm, **Creative Co., Inc.**
Art Director, **Jennifer Larson Morrow**
Designer, **Nancy Dean Chamberlain**
Illustrator, **Dan Franklin**
Copywriter, **Chemeketa Community College**
Client, **Chemeketa Community College**
Four colors and varnish on 100-lb.
Productolith gloss

2
Design Firm, **Richardson or Richardson**
Art Director, **Forrest Richardson/**
Valerie Richardson
Designer, **Forrest Richardson/Valerie Richardson**
Client, **Phoenix Velodrome Association**
Two colors

This piece is bound and enclosed in a Black Coroplast cover.

1
Design Firm, **Patterson Wood Partners**
Art Director, **Tom Wood**
Designer, **Tom Wood/Carrie Berman**
Illustrator, **Karen Knorr**
Copywriter, **Mary Anne Costello**
Client, **Louis Dreyfus Property Group**
Six colors on Ikonofix matte

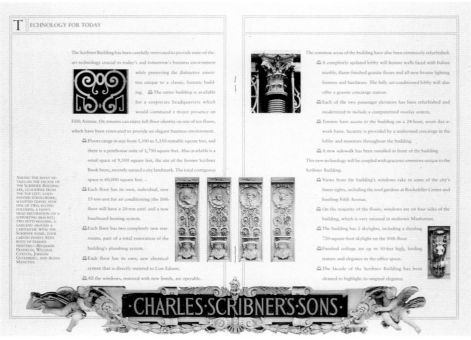

1
Design Firm, **Patterson Wood Partners**
Art Director, **Tom Wood**
Designer, **Tom Wood**
Photographer, **Tom Leighton**
Copywriter, **Mary Anne Costello**
Client, **Louis Dreyfus Property Group**
Six colors on Simpson Evergreen/
Consolidated Reflections

2
Design Firm, **Stillman Design Associates**
Art Director, **Linda Stillman**
Designer, **Connie Circosta**
Copywriter, **Jan Billingsley**
Client, **Cushman & Wakefield**
Four colors on Lustro Dull

*Architectural details from the Scribner Building were
photographed and used as spot illustrations for
this brochure.*

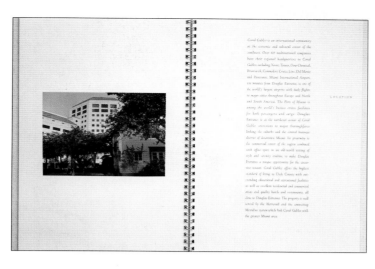

Coral Gables es una comunidad internacional en el centro económico y cultural del sureste. Más de 60 compañías multinacionales tienen su sede regional en Coral Gables, incluyendo Xerox, Texaco, Dow Chemical, Brunswick, Panasonic, Del Monte y Commodore Cruise Line. El Aeropuerto Internacional de Miami, a solo diez minutos de Douglas Entrance, es uno de los aeropuertos más importantes del mundo, con vuelos diarios a las principales ciudades de Europa, Norte, Centro y Sur America. El puerto de Miami, con sus facilidades para cruceros y cargo, se encuentra entre los más concurridos del mundo. Douglas Entrance se encuentra ubicada en la esquina noreste de Coral Gables, con fácil acceso a las principales arterias que enlazan los suburbios residenciales con el centro financiero de Miami. Su cercanía al centro comercial de la región junto con la elegancia de su estilo europeo hacen de Douglas Entrance una oportunidad extraordinaria para el inquilino ejecutivo. Coral Gables ofrece el nivel de vida más alto del Condado Dade, con excelentes facilidades educacionales y recreativas, así como estupendas zonas residenciales y comerciales, hoteles y restaurantes de la más alta categoría, todos cercanos a Douglas Entrance. La propiedad es fácilmente accesible por Metrorail y la red de autobuses que une a Coral Gables con el área metropolitana de Miami.

UBICACIÓN

1
Design Firm, **Patterson Wood Partners**
Art Director, **Tom Wood**
Designer, **Tom Wood**
Photographer, **Tom Wood/Phil Brodate**
Copywriter, **Mary Anne Costello**
Client, **Louis Dreyfus Property Group**
Six colors on Mohawk Superfine handmade paper

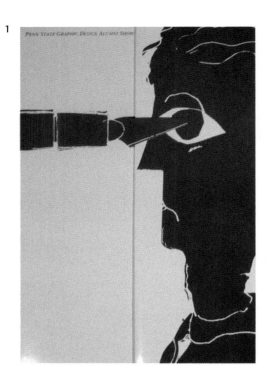

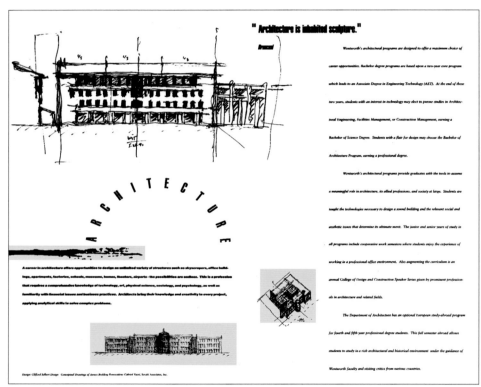

1

Design Firm, **Sommese Design**
Art Director, **Lanny Sommese**
Designer, **Kristin Sommese**
Illustrator, **Lanny Sommese**
Copywriter, **Lanny Sommese**
Client, **School of Visual Arts, Penn State**
One color on Kromekote

As this brochure is opened, the exacto blade is pulled
from the eye. The gimmick is achieved both by the
accordion fold of the brochure and the fact that the
blade of the exacto knife is die-cut so that it can
overlap one of the folds and be inserted into a slot
cut into the eye. Once inserted, it becomes a
fastening device.

2

Design Firm, **Clifford Selbert Design**
Art Director, **Clifford Selbert**
Designer, **Robin Perkins**
Illustrator, **Gabriel Yaari**
Client, **Wentworth Institute of Technology**
Two colors, spot varnish on Consort Royal Silk

50   THE BEST OF BROCHURE DESIGN

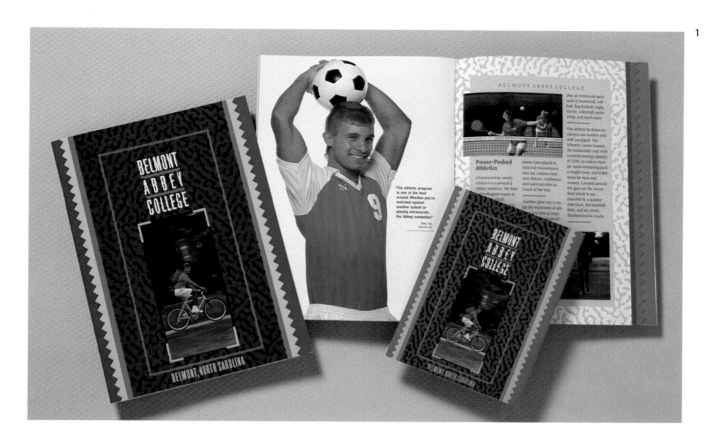

1
Design Firm, **Steve Galit Associates, Inc.**
Art Director, **Christine Pearson**
Designer, **Christine Pearson**
Photographer, **Roger Ball**
Client, **Belmont Abbey College**
Four colors and varnish on LOE gloss

2
Design Firm, **Steve Galit Associates,Inc.**
Art Director, **Christine Pearson**
Designer, **Christine Pearson**
Photographer, **Roger Ball**
Client, **WIX DANA**
Five colors and varnish on 100-lb. Vintage gloss
cover and text

1
Design Firm, **Steve Galit Associates,Inc.**
Art Director, **Steve Galit**
Designer, **Steve Galit**
Photographer, **Roger Ball**
Client, **Duke Power Co.**
Four process colors/one PMS color on American
Eagle Web with laminated cover

2
Design Firm, **Steve Galit Associates,Inc.**
Art Director, **Steve Galit**
Designer, **Steve Galit**
Photographer, **Roger Ball**
Client, **Duke Power Company**
Four process colors/one PMS color on American
Eagle Web with laminated cover

1
Design Firm, **Steve Galit Associates, Inc.**
Art Director, **Christine Pearson**
Designer, **Christine Pearson**
Photographer, **Ron Chapple**
Copywriter, **Ted Matthews**
Client, **Springs Industries**
Five colors and varnish on LOE gloss

2
Design Firm, **Steve Galit Associates, Inc.**
Art Director, **Christine Pearson**
Designer, **Christine Pearson**
Photographer, **Roger Ball**
Client, **Springs Industries**
Five colors and varnish on Ikonofix cover and text

PRODUCT BOOKLETS

1
Design Firm, **MartinRoss Design**
Art Director, **Martin Skoro/Ross Rezac**
Designer, **Martin Skoro/Ross Rezac**
Photographer, **Ben Saltzman**
Copywriter, **Wardrop Murtaugh Temple**
Client, **Consolidated Papers, Inc.**
Ten colors on Centura

WHEN IT
COMES
TO TOY
SOLDIERS,
A SCULPTOR'S
SKILLFUL OR
UNIQUE
ATTENTION
COMBINED
WITH CAREFULL
AND DETAILED
PAINTING
NOT ONLY
ENHANCES
VALUE UPON
COMPLETION
BUT AS THE
PIECES AGE
OVER YEARS
AND DECADES
THEY BECOME
VALUED AND
CHARISHED
COLLECTIBLES.

CENTURA
ESSENTIALLY
HOLDS A
MIRROR TO
THE ORIGINAL
ART OR
PHOTOGRAPH.
EVEN IN
THE SMOKE
OF BATTLE,
NO DETAIL
IS LOST AND
JUST AS
MANY OF THE
MINIATURES
END THEIR
DAYS IN
A MUSEUM,
IT IS NO
COINCIDENCE
THAT CENTURA
IS OF SIMILAR
ARCHIVAL
QUALITY.

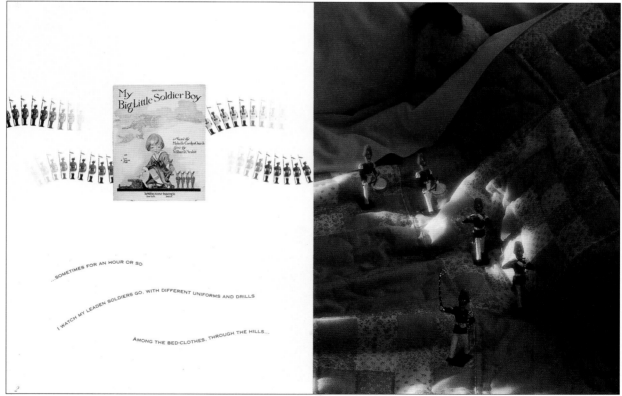

...SOMETIMES FOR AN HOUR OR SO

I WATCH MY LEADEN SOLDIERS GO, WITH DIFFERENT UNIFORMS AND DRILLS

AMONG THE BED-CLOTHES, THROUGH THE HILLS...

1
Design Firm, **Alan Chan Design Co.**
Art Director, **Alan Chan/Alvin Chan**
Designer, **Alan Chan/Alvin Chan/Cetric Leung**
Photographer, **Raymond Wong/stock photos**
Client, **James Wong Productions, Ltd.**
Six colors on art card, art paper

This is an introductory and lyric brochure that comes in a box together with a compact disc entitled "The Four Chinese Beauties," performed by Hung Sin Lui, one of the most famous singers in China.

因為女媧出塞、鄉愁的四首作品，我都好奇知之甚詳……

王德出塞、鄉愁纏綿至海悠哀，女姐的歌述中忙，中情夢知之甚詳……

古曲、是女媧和香之後、後唱再生生活實有快感……

「明月幾、用跨人耳內線音再的古曲、用製幾幾以家東員……

曲曲情、用跨人耳內線音再的古曲、用製幾幾以家東員……

民用用製此配上別製、刻製幾幾現製再製幾出塞外少數……

哀秋鄉配女以家配女、配女配上女文東再製再製再製再製……

形

音樂

這首歌，道盡天下女人被男人欺負的綿長悶恨。

音樂設計，用上了較現代的配器法，還加上風雷電聲音效果，是戲劇化的音樂處理。

古曲「夜深沉」跟着，句哀恨交纏的「倒板」，「連七都「淒」字之後，再七個「嘆」字，把對負心人的怨訴都顯露出來。

中段的「黃慢板連序」，是紅譚女數十年演唱生涯罕通百像積聚的功力，「綿綿長恨」句的拉腔，展示了女姥精髓。

女姐清唱的「乙反木魚」，錯彩得豪量難以細出萬。

長
恨歌

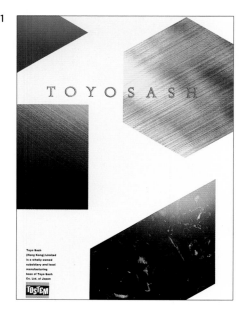

T O Y O S A S H

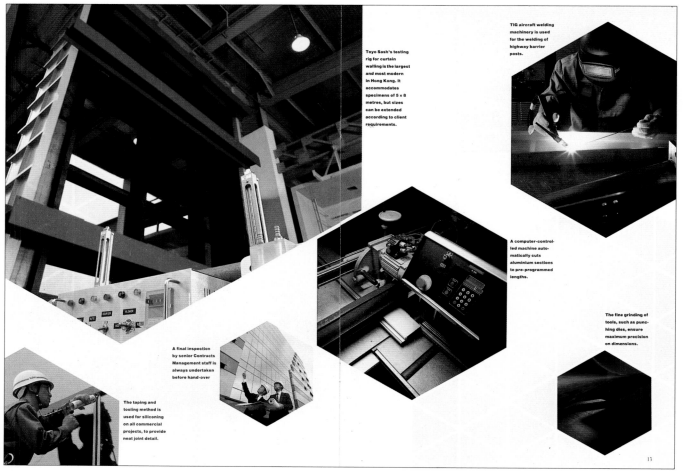

1
Design Firm, **Alan Chan Design Co.**
Art Director, **Alan Chan/Alvin Chan**
Designer, **Alan Chan/Alvin Chan/Cetric Leung**
Photographer, **Sandy Lee**
Client, **Toyo Sash Ltd.**
Five colors on matte paper, art card

1
Design Firm, **Chermayeff & Geismar, Inc.**
Art Director, **Steff Geissbuhler**
Designer, **Bill Anton**
Illustrator, **Stephen Alcorn**
Copywriter, **Rose DeNeve**
Client, **Crane & Co.**
Seven colors on Crane

2
Design Firm, **Chermayeff & Geismar, Inc.**
Art Director, **Tom Geismar**
Designer, **Bill Anton**
Copywriter, **Paul Rosenthal**
Client, **Westvaco**
Four colors on Celesta

1
Design Firm, **Taylor/Christian Advertising, Inc.**
Designer, **Roger Christian**
Photographer, **Swain Edens**
Copywriter, **David Allen**
Client, **Clarke Checks**
Four color process

2
Design Firm, **Morla Design**
Art Director, **Jennifer Morla**
Designer, **Jennifer Morla/Jeanette Aramburu**
Illustrator, **John Mattos**
Mezzotints: Heliogramme
Photographer, **Michael LaMotte**
Copywriter, **George Cruys**
Client, **Simpson Paper Co.**
Four process colors, die-cut, foil stamped, and
thermography on Valley Forge Parchment

1
Design Firm, **Bernhardt Fudyma Design Group**
Art Director, **Craig Bernhardt/Janice Fudyma**
Designer, **Iris Brown**
Copywriter, **Barry Bohrer**
Client, **Gilbert Paper Co.**
Four process colors/three PMS colors on Gilbert
Oxford and Gilbert Gilclear

1
Design Firm, **Pat Gorman Design/
Manhattan Design**
Art Director, **Pat Gorman**
Designer, **Pat Gorman**
Photographer, **Virginia Liberatore/stock**
Copywriter, **Manhattan Design**
Client, **Robert A. Clair Co., Inc.**
Four process colors/two flourescent colors on
12-pt. coated

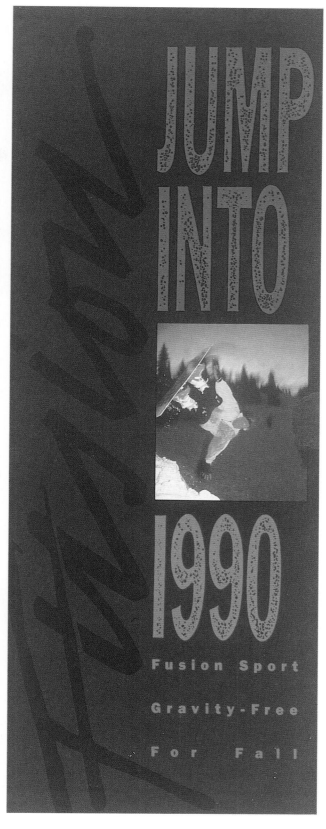

1
Design Firm, **Pat Gorman Design/**
Manhattan Design
Art Director, **Pat Gorman**
Designer, **Pat Gorman**
Photographer, **Jennifer Levy/Aaron Strong/**
Team Russel/stock
Copywriter, **Manhattan Design**
Client, **Robert A. Clair Co., Inc.**
Four process colors/matte black and spot varnish
on 80-lb. dull coated

1
Design Firm, **Charles S. Anderson Design Co.**
Art Director, **Daniel Olson/Charles S. Anderson/**
Haley Johnson
Designer, **Daniel Olson**
Photographer, **Dave Bausman**
Copywriter, **Lisa Pemrick**
Client, **Hollywood Paramount Pictures**
Six colors on Zanders Kromelux (cover), konorex
dull (text), and Three Crowns White (fly sheets)

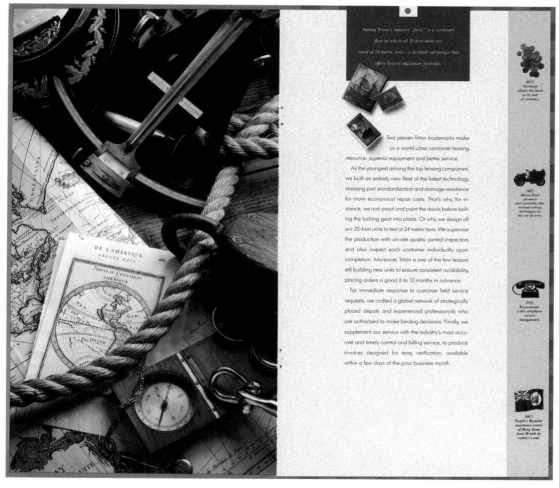

1
Design Firm, **Jamie Davison Design, Inc.**
Art Director, **Jamie Davison**
Designer, **Jamie Davison/Rita Damore**
Photographer, **Henrik Kam**
Copywriter, **Lindsay Beaman**
Client, **Triton Container Corp.**
Eight colors and varnish

1
Design Firm, **The Kuester Group**
Art Director, **Kevin B. Kuester/Brent Marmo**
Designer, **Bob Goebel**
Photographer, **Philip Porcella**
Copywriter, **David Forney**
Client, **Potlatch Corp., Northwest Paper Division**
Four process colors/one match color and one gloss
varnish on 80/100-lb. text and 80/100-lb. cover

2
Design Firm, **The Kuester Group**
Art Director, **Kevin B. Kuester**
Designer, **Bob Goebel**
Copywriter, **David Forney**
Client, **Potlatch Corp., Northwest Paper Division**
Four process colors/two match colors and one
gloss varnish on Potlatch Karma Bright White 65-
lb. cover, 100-lb. text

Cover is blind-embossed.

1
Design Firm, **The Kuester Group**
Art Director, **Kevin B. Kuester/Brent Marmo**
Designer, **Brent Marmo**
Copywriter, **David Forney**
Client, **Potlatch Corp., Northwest Paper Division**
Ten colors on Quintessence gloss and dull

1
Design Firm, **The Kuester Group**
Art Director, **Kevin B. Kuester/Brent Marmo**
Designer, **Brent Marmo**
Illustrator, **Kevin Sprouls/Mike Lizama/**
John Kleber
Photographer, **Dewitt Jones/Geoff Kern/**
Clint Clemens
Copywriter, **David Forney/Craig Caldwell**
Client, **Nissan Motor Corp., Infiniti Division**
Four process colors, dull tint, and gloss varnish on
Vintage gloss

2
Design Firm, **The Kuester Group**
Art Director, **Kevin B. Kuester**
Designer, **Bob Goebel**
Photographer, **Greg Booth + Associates**
Copywriter, **David Forney**
Client, **Potlatch Corp., Northwest Paper Division**
Four process colors, one match, and one gloss
varnish on Potlatch Vintage gloss 100-lb. cover
and 100-lb. text

1
Design Firm, **The Kuester Group**
Art Director, **Kevin B. Kuester**
Designer, **Tim Sauer**
Illustrator, **Margret Huber**
Photographer, **Thomas Twining Photography**
Copywriter, **David Forney**
Client, **Potlatch Corp., Northwest Paper Division**
Nine colors on Potlatch Northwest gloss

1
Design Firm, **The Kuester Group**
Art Director, **Kevin B. Kuester**
Designer, **Tim Sauer**
Photographer, **Ben Salzman**
Copywriter, **David Forney**
Client, **Potlatch Corp., Northwest Paper Division**
Six colors on Potlatch Northwest gloss

2
Design Firm, **Tharp Did It**
Art Director, **Rick Tharp**
Designer, **Rick Tharp**
Illustrator, **James Lamarche/Littlejohn/**
Sharron O'Neil/Rick Tharp/Kim Tomlinson
Photographer, **Franklin Avery/Stan Cacitti**
Copywriter, **Charles Drummond**
Client, **Mirassou Vineyards, Seagram Classics**
Nine colors and gold foil on Simpson
Gainsborough, Wire O binding

design and communication for the W.C.

on Champion Kromekote 2000

Little has changed in the workings of the W.C. during the last century except to bring the overhead water cistern down from its lofty perch, thereby eliminating the pull and chain.

*Water Closet

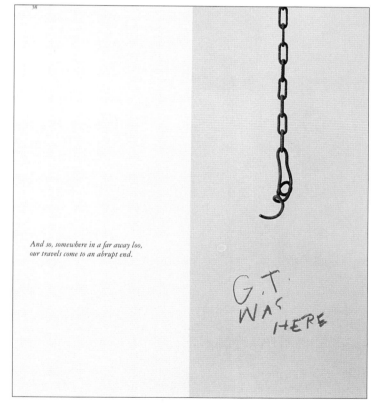

And so, somewhere in a far away loo, our travels come to an abrupt end.

1
Design Firm, **George Tscherny, Inc.**
Art Director, **George Tscherny**
Designer, **George Tscherny**
Photographer, **George Tscherny**
Copywriter, **George Tscherny**
Client, **Champion International**
Six colors on Champion Kromekote 2000

1
Design Firm, **Morla Design**
Art Director, **Jennifer Morla**
Designer, **Jennifer Morla**
Photographer, **David Robin**
Copywriter, **Lisa Tarlington**
Client, **Bradmill, Inc.**
Six colors on Speckletone Kraft

1
Design Firm, **Morla Design**
Art Director, **Jennifer Morla**
Designer, **Jennifer Morla**
Illustrator, **Jennifer Morla/Erik Watts**
Photographer, **Thomas Heinser**
Copywriter, **Jennifer Morla/Julie Klee**
Client, **Levi Strauss & Co.**

1

1
Design Firm, **Morla Design**
Art Director, **Jennifer Morla**
Designer, **Jennifer Morla**
Photographer, **Elaine Keenan**
Copywriter, **NY Times (1927), LA Times (1929)**
Client, **Common Man's Apparel**
Four process colors/one PMS on Parchtone
Natural cover

*The unique use of four color process on parchment
stock created the newspaper look; matte texture is
created with a fifth color.*

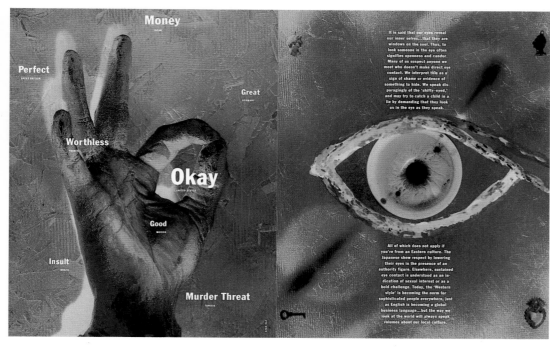

2

1
Design Firm, **The Weller Institute for the Cure of Design, Inc.**
Art Director, **Don Weller**
Designer, **Don Weller**
Photographer, **Don Weller**
Copywriter, **Thomas McGuane**
Client, **National Cutting Horse Association**
Four process colors and varnish on Cameo

2
Design Firm, **Frankfurt Gips Balkind**
Art Director, **Kent Hunter/Aubrey Balkind**
Designer, **Kent Hunter/Ruth Diener**
Illustrator, **Elwood Smith/J. Otto Siebold/ San Simon/Tim Lewis**
Photographer, **Scott Morgan/Stan Gaz**
Copywriter, **Danny Abelson/Cindy Ris**
Client, **Simpson**
Seven Simpson paper grades

1

2

1
Design Firm, **Hornall Anderson Design Works**
Art Director, **Jack Anderson**
Designer, **Jack Anderson/Juliet Shen/David Bates**
Illustrator, **John and Leilani Fortune**
Photographer, **Mark Burnside**
Copywriter, **Dan Balazs**
Client, **Diadora USA**
Four process colors/one PMS and a varnish on
Lustro gloss book

2
Design Firm, **Hornall Anderson Design Works**
Art Director, **Jack Anderson**
Designer, **Jack Anderson/Juliet Shen**
Illustrator, **John Fortune/Tim Killian/HADW**
Photographer, **Mark Burnside**
Copywriter, **Dan Balazs**
Client, **Diadora USA**
Four process colors/one PMS and a varnish
Starwhite Vicksburg (cover), Lustro gloss
book (text)

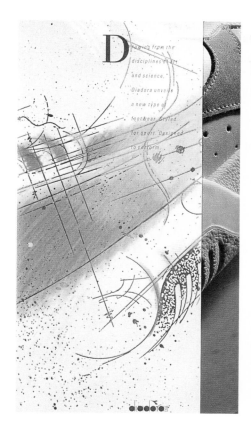

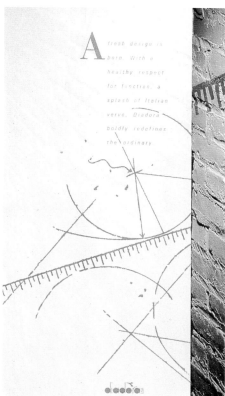

1
Design Firm, **Hornall Anderson Design Works**
Art Director, **Jack Anderson**
Designer, **Jack Anderson/Heidi Hatlestad**
Illustrator, **John Fortune/Tim Killian/HADW**
Photographer, **Mark Burnside/Todd Pearson**
Copywriter, **Dan Balazs**
Client, **Diadora USA**
Four process colors/one PMS and a varnish

2
Design Firm, **Hornall Anderson Design Works**
Art Director, **Jack Anderson**
Designer, **Jack Anderson/Cheri Huber**
Illustrator, **Nancy Gellos**
Photographer, **Mark Burnside**
Copywriter, **Dan Balazs**
Client, **Diadora USA**
Four process colors/one PMS and a varnish

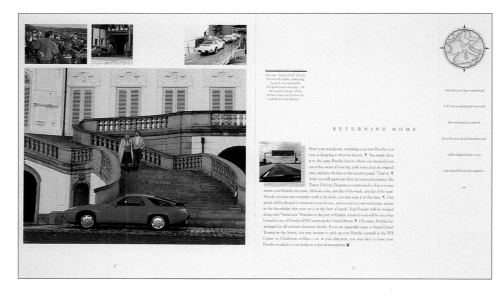

2

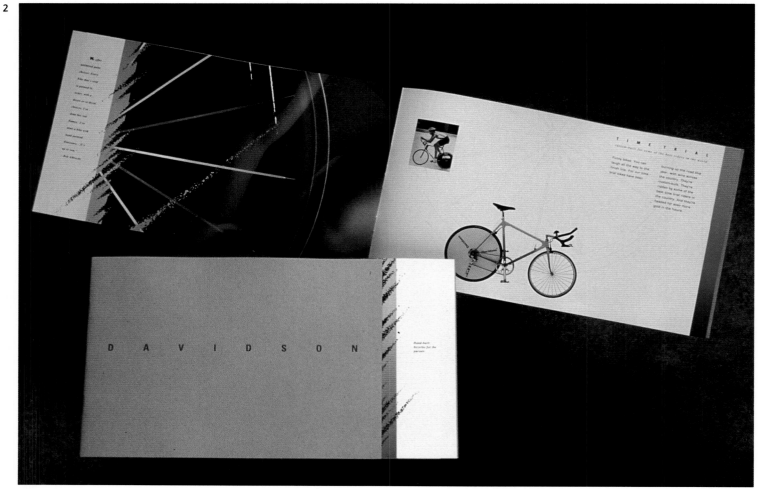

1
Design Firm, **Hornall Anderson Design Works**
Art Director, **Luann Bice**
Designer, **Luann Bice**
Illustrator, **Heidi Hatlestad/Mary Hermes**
Photographer, **Kai Scheufler**
Copywriter, **David McFadden**
Client, **Porsche Cars North America**

2
Design Firm, **Hornall Anderson Design Works**
Art Director, **Jack Anderson**
Designer, **Jack Anderson/Jani Drewfs/Mary Hermes**
Illustrator, **David Bates/Scott McDougall (airbrush)**
Photographer, **Tom Collicott**
Copywriter, **Pamela Mason-Davey**
Client, **Davidson Cycles**
Six colors on Kraft Centura

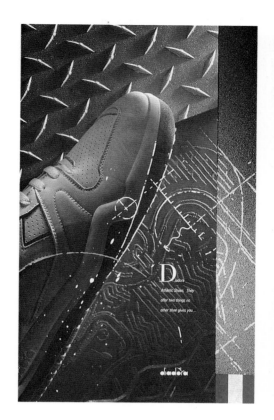

1
Design Firm, **Hornall Anderson Design Works**
Art Director, **Jack Anderson**
Designer, **Jack Anderson/Juliet Shen/Mary Hermes**
Illustrator, **John Fortune/HADW**
Photographer, **Mark Burnside**
Copywriter, **Steve Sandoz**
Client, **Diadora USA**
Four process colors/one PMS and a varnish on Vintage gloss

2
Design Firm, **Pinkhaus Design Corp.**
Art Director, **Joel Fuller**
Designer, **Mark Cantor/Lisa Ashworth**
Photographer, **Bruce Miller/Brad Miller**
Copywriter, **Frank Cunningham**
Client, **Austin Rover Cars of North America**
Six colors on Consolidated Reflections

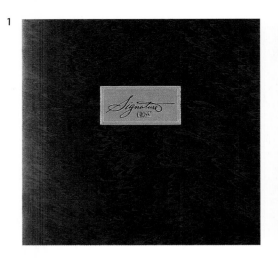

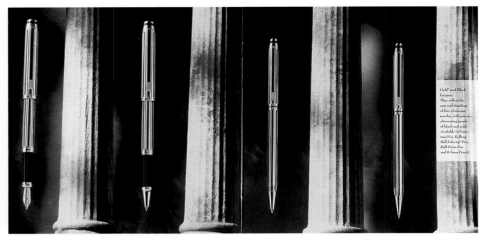

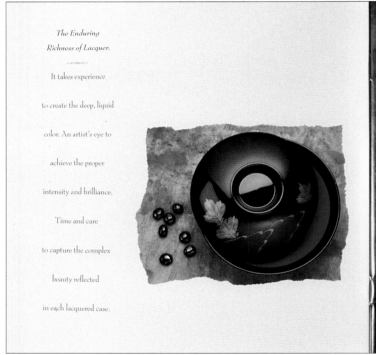

1
Design Firm, **Hill Holliday Design**
Art Director, **Vic Cevoli**
Designer, **Tricia McMahon**
Copywriter, **Neill Ray**
Client, **A.T. Cross Co.**
Four process colors on Reflections Paper

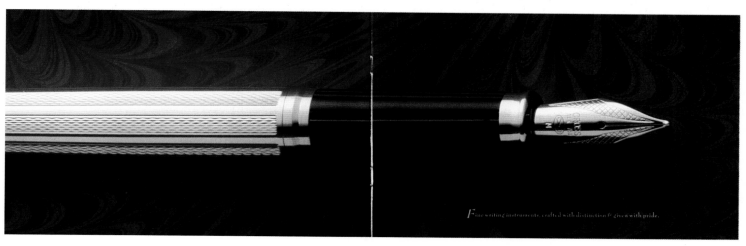

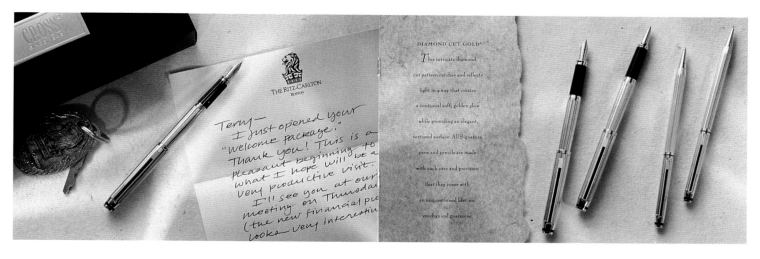

1
Design Firm, **Hill Holliday Design**
Art Director, **Vic Cevoli**
Designer, **Tricia McMahon**
Photographer, **Myron**
Copywriter, **Neill Ray**
Client, **A.T. Cross Co.**
Four process colors on Reflections Paper

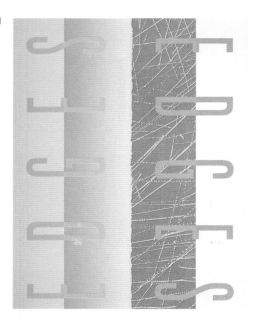

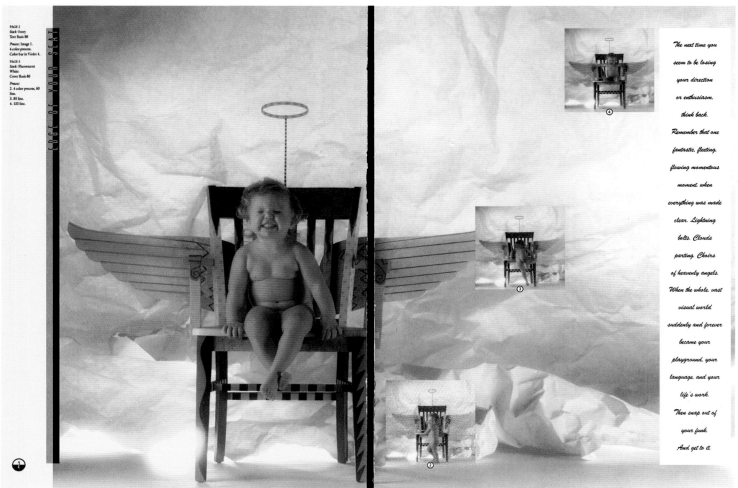

1
Design Firm, **Muller & Co.**
Art Director, **John Muller**
Designer, **Muller & Co.**
Copywriter, **David Marks**
Client, **Strathmore Paper Co.**
Six colors on Strathmore Pastelle

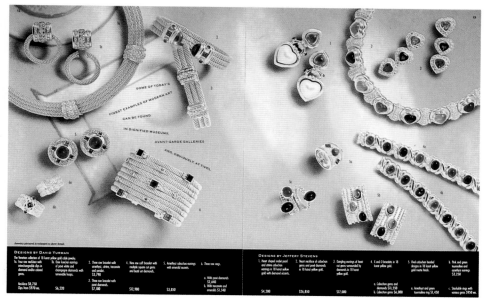

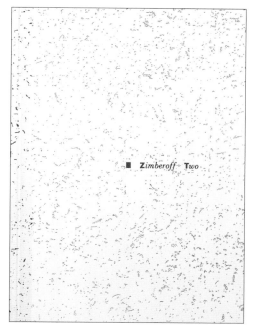

1
Design Firm, **Muller & Co.**
Art Director, **Jane Weeks/John Muller**
Designer, **Jane Weeks**
Photographer, **Mike Regnier**
Copywriter, **David Marks**
Client, **Tivol Jewelry**
Five colors and aqueous coating on
Kromekote B Vintage

2
Design Firm, **Butler Kosh Brooks**
Art Director, **Carlos Cordova**
Designer, **Carlos Cordova**
Photographer, **Tom Zimberoff**
Client, **Champion Papers**
Six colors on Champion Kromekote 2000

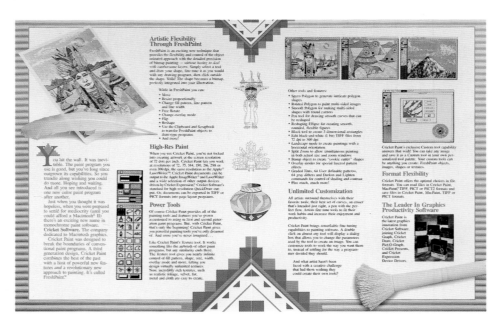

1
Design Firm, **RGF&L**
Art Director, **Patricia Fox Sussman**
Designer, **Patricia Fox Sussman**
Photographer, **Jim Green**
Client, **Cricket Software**
Five colors on 80-lb. Vintage Velvet cover

2
Design Firm, **Creative Co., Inc.**
Art Director, **Jennifer Larsen Morrow**
Designer, **Joy Eno**
Photographer, **Barrett Rudich**
Copywriter, **Michael Perman**
Client, **Great American Herb Co.**
Four color process on 80-lb. dull book

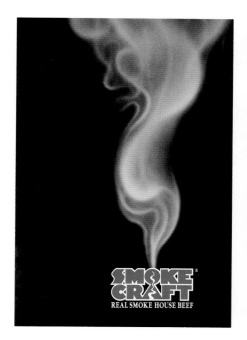

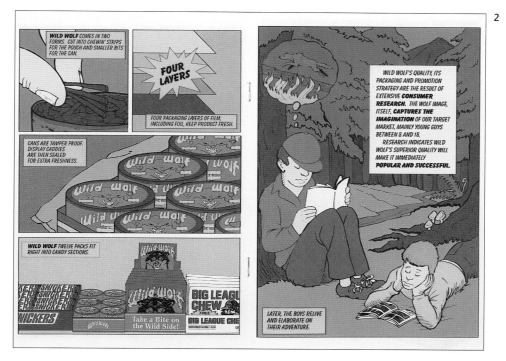

1
Design Firm, **Creative Co., Inc.**
Art Director, **Jennifer Larsen Morrow**
Designer, **Cathie Von**
Photographer, **Mike Dahlstrom**
Copywriter, **Michael Perman**
Client, **Curtis Burns Meat Snacks**
Four colors plus on 80-lb. gloss cover (premium)

2
Design Firm, **Creative Co., Inc.**
Art Director, **Jennifer Larsen Morrow**
Designer, **Mike Satern/Laura Trammel**
Illustrator, **Barry Nichols**
Copywriter, **Michael Perman**
Client, **Curtis Burns Meat Snacks**
Four colors on 80-lb. Productolithe book gloss
(cover) and Hammermill book vellum white
opaque 70-lb. (inside)

1
Design Firm, **Sayles Graphic Design**
Art Director, **John Sayles**
Designer, **John Sayles**
Illustrator, **John Sayles**
Photographer, **Bill Nellans**
Copywriter, **Julie Summerlot**
Client, **Gilbert Paper**
Five colors on Gilbert Oxford

An unusual effect is created for this paper promotion by intermingling photographs and illustrations printed with four flourescent colors instead of traditional process colors.

2
Design Firm, **Sayles Graphic Design**
Art Director, **John Sayles**
Designer, **John Sayles**
Illustrator, **John Sayles**
Copywriter, **Wendy Lyons**
Client, **Maytag Co.**
Five colors on James River Tuscan Terra

The second part of this two-part mailing invites readers to "Plug into the Power" and actually lights up when the plug is inserted into an outlet.

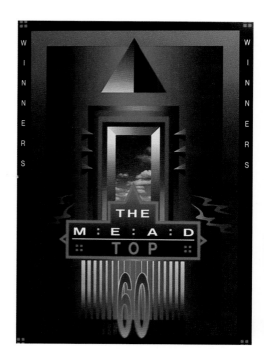

1
Design Firm, **Pangborn Design, Ltd.**
Art Director, **Dominic Pangborn**
Designer, **Dominic Pangborn**
Illustrator, **Han-Eung Kim**
Copywriter, **The Mead Co.**
Client, **The Mead Co.**
Four process colors, dense black, and aqueous
coating (cover) on Mead Offset Enamel
100-lb. text

2
Design Firm, **Knoth & Meads**
Art Director, **Jose Serrano**
Designer, **Tracy Sabin**
Illustrator, **Tracy Sabin**
Copywriter, **John Kuraoka**
Client, **McMillin Communities**
Four process colors on Speckletone

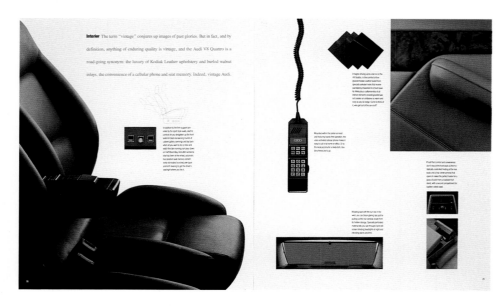

1
Design Firm, **SHR Design Communications**
Art Director, **Barry Shepard/Karin Burklein Arnold**
Designer, **Karin Burklein Arnold**
Illustrator, **Carol Hughes**
Copywriter, **Steve Hutchison**
Client, **Audi of America, Inc.**
Six colors on 100-lb. Golden Cask text and cover

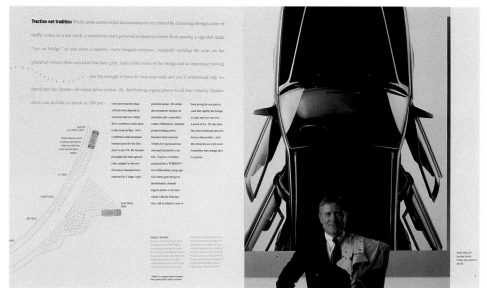

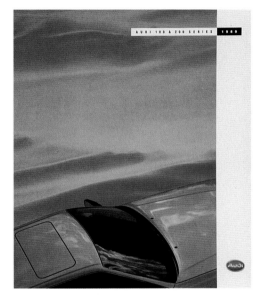

1
Design Firm, **SHR Design Communications**
Art Director, **Barry Shepard/Karin Burklein Arnold/Steve Ditko**
Designer, **Karin Burklein Arnold/Miles Abernethy**
Illustrator, **Carol Hughes**
Photographer, **Rick Rusing**
Copywriter, **Steve Hutchinson**
Client, **Audi of America, Inc.**

2
Design Firm, **SHR Design Communications**
Art Director, **Barry Shepard**
Designer, **Karin Burklein Arnold/Steve Ditko/ Doug Reeder/Barry Shepard**
Illustrator, **Carol Hughes/Roland Dahlquist/ Rick Kirkman**
Photographer, **Rick Rusing**
Copywriter, **Steve Hogan**
Client, **Audi of America, Inc.**
Six colors on 100-lb. Golden Cask text and cover

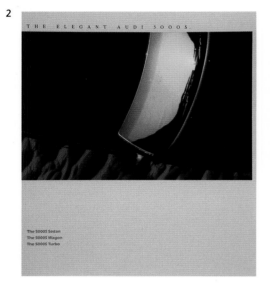

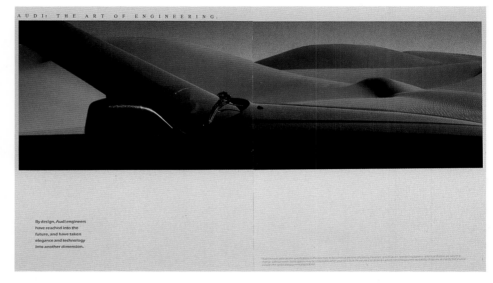

1
Design Firm, **SHR Design Communications**
Art Director, **Barry Shepard/**
Karin Burklein Arnold
Designer, **Barry Shepard**
Photographer, **Rick Rusing/Rodney Rascona**
Copywriter, **Steve Hutchinson**
Client, **Audi of America, Inc.**
Six colors on 90-lb. Reflections book, Kromekote
10pt C2S, 70-lb. Curtis Brightwater Riblaid
text (flysheet)

2
Design Firm, **SHR Design Communications**
Art Director, **Barry Shepard**
Designer, **Barry Shepard**
Illustrator, **Wayne Wetford**
Photographer, **Bob Bender/Rick Gayle/**
Rick Rusing
Copywriter, **George Thorne**
Client, **Audi of America, Inc.**
Six colors on Ikonolux 92.5-lb. cover, 100-lb. text

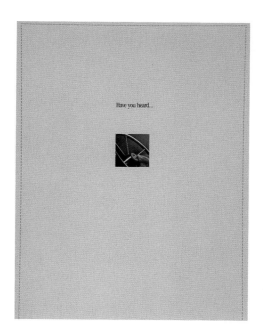

Have you heard...

Why does it take four times longer to build a Cobalt boat than most? Because 250 good Cobalt people build it by hand.

The story of how Cobalt boats are built is a magnificent one. It is about a family of people, deeply committed to excellence, who believe their purpose is to bring as much enjoyment as possible to their Cobalt owners.

There's really no better place to begin than with the making of the hull itself. Did you know, for example, many boat hulls are built in eight hours or less? In Neodesha, it takes three to five days. Much like fine wines which better please the palate after proper aging in their casks, Cobalt hulls are allowed to properly cure in their molds. This properly strengthens the hulls, which prevents warping. The result is a longer lasting, more beautiful finish.

After curing, each hull is weighed to verify the correct balance of resin to fiberglass. A significant variation would make the hull too brittle, or too flexible. The hull thickness is then measured with a sonic testing device in at least 50 places. A boat hull is only as strong as its weakest point, and Cobalt craftsmen demand consistent hull thickness.

The hull is now ready to be subjected to the glare of the powerful lights in the Quality Control Room, where white-gloved inspectors scrutinize each hull for subtle blemishes the untrained eye would never notice. For that matter, everyone at Cobalt is involved in quality control. Anyone, at any time, who spots any defect—no matter how small—feels compelled to get it right.

On a Cobalt, though, many of the more important quality features you can't even see. Aluminum plates are strategically placed under the deck to provide metal surfaces to which handrails are secured. A Cobalt owner will never be caught standing at the dock, handrail in hand, as his boat drifts away, because the handrails were fastened only to fiberglass. Many components (like cabinet doors) are also double-fastened. If two pieces are glued together, they are also doweled, screwed or stapled as well...

This is only the beginning of the Cobalt story. To fully appreciate the difference, test drive other new boats. Then go for a ride in a Cobalt. Experience the difference for yourself...It's as if 250 craftsmen were right there with you...all the way...

I C O N

The Lumen

The Lumen is a two-way, bookshelf-sized speaker that has a big, compelling sound. It may be the only speaker you will ever need. It is also an excellent choice for those who have limited space, need speakers for a second system, or for surround-sound applications. And their low price can ease the pain for those of you just getting into high end audio.

The Lumen is built to the same high standards as the Parsec, our flagship speaker. It is a very satisfying speaker capable of reproducing all but the lowest notes of the tuba, bassoon, bass, piano, and organ.

You may be suprised by the low price. By selling our speakers directly to you we can afford to use the very best components from around the world — components usually reserved for speakers costing over $1000. Icon speakers feature metal-dome tweeters from Norway; polypropylene woofers from Denmark; polypropylene capacitors from France (made especially for high end audio applications); polystyrene bypass capacitors from the U.S., internal wire from AudioQuest™; and two pair of gold Tiffany 5-way binding posts set up for optional bi-wiring.

1
Design Firm, **SHR Design Communications**
Art Director, **Barry Shepard**
Designer, **Steve Ditko**
Photographer, **Rick Rusing**
Copywriter, **George Thorne**
Client, **Cobalt Boats**
Six colors on 80-lb. Ikonofix cover, 70-lb. text

2
Design Firm, **Clifford Selbert Design**
Art Director, **Clifford Selbert**
Designer, **Lynn Riddle Waller**
Photographer, **Susie Cushner**
Copywriter, **David Fokos/Allison Bartlett**
Client, **Icon Acoustics**
Four process colors/one PMS color on Elephant Hide LOE

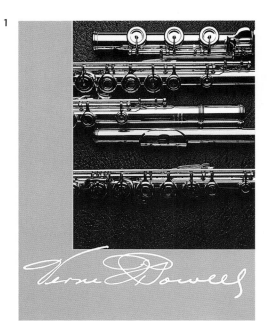

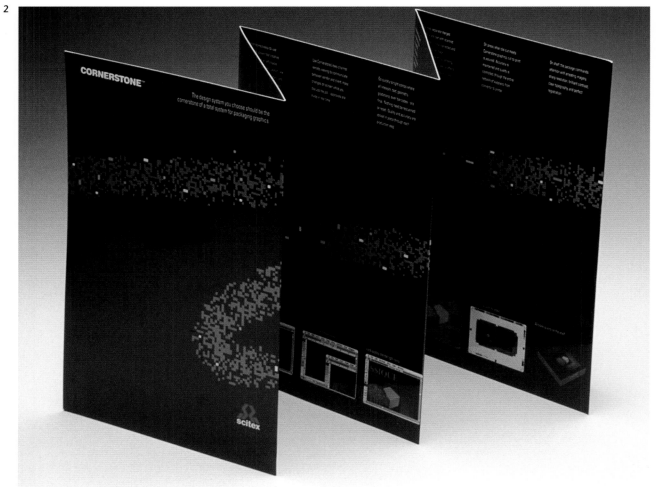

1
Design Firm, **Portfolio**
Art Director, **Wendy Terry**
Photographer, **Lou Jones**
Copywriter, **Steve Wasser**
Client, **Verne Q. Powell Flutes**
Four process colors/one PMS/one Toyo and gloss
spot varnish on 80-lb. Vintage gloss cover

2
Design Firm, **Kollberg/Johnson Associates**
Art Director, **Gary Kollberg**
Designer, **Michael Carr**
Copywriter, **Gary Kollberg/Michael Carr**
Client, **Scitex**
Eight colors on 100-lb. Lustrogloss cover

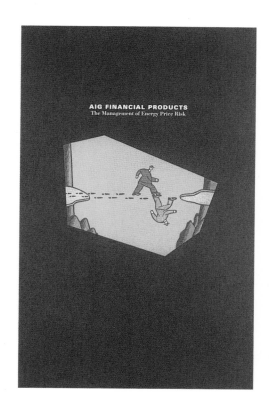

1
Design Firm, **Bernhardt Fudyma Design Group**
Art Director, **Craig Bernhardt**
Designer, **Frank Baseman/Craig Bernhardt**
Illustrator, **Brian Cronin**
Copywriter, **Rena Grossfield**
Client, **AIG Financial Products**
Six colors on Strathmore Rhododendron,
Reflections text

2
Design Firm, **Bernhardt Fudyma Design Group**
Art Director, **Craig Bernhardt/Janice Fudyma**
Designer, **Ron Shankweiler**
Photographer, **Dick Frank**
Client, **Fluid Conditioning Products**
Four process colors

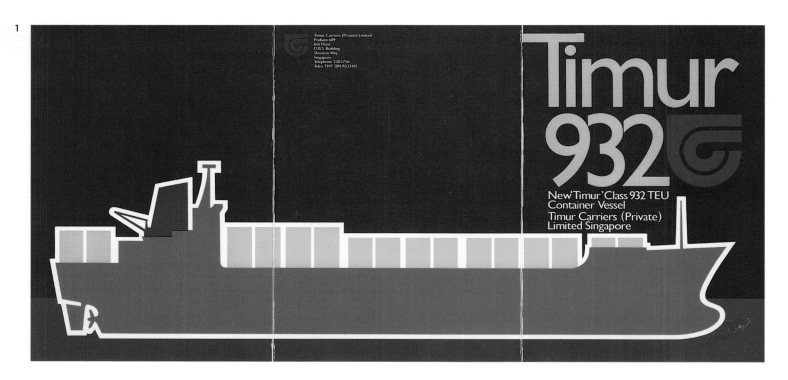

Timur Carriers (Private) Limited
Podium 609
6th Floor
D.B.S. Building
Shenton Way
Singapore
Telephone 2203756
Telex TNT SIN RS23415

Timur 932

New 'Timur' Class 932 TEU
Container Vessel
Timur Carriers (Private)
Limited Singapore

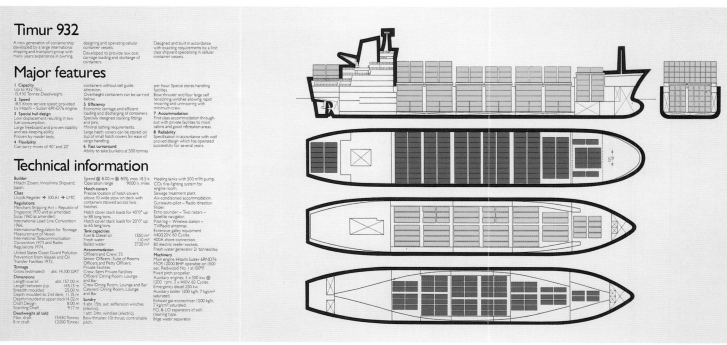

Timur 932

A new generation of containership developed by a large international shipping and transport group with many years experience in owning, designing and operating cellular container vessels. Developed to provide low cost carriage loading and discharge of containers. Designed and built in accordance with exacting requirements by a first class shipyard specialising in cellular container vessels.

Major features

1 Capacity
Up to 932 TEU.
15,430 Tonnes Deadweight.
2 Speed
18.5 Knots service speed provided by Hitachi – Sulzer 6RND76 engine.
3 Special hull design
Low displacement resulting in low fuel consumption.
Large freeboard and proven stability and sea-keeping ability.
Proven by model tests.
4 Flexibility
Can carry mixes of 40' and 20' containers without cell guide alteration.
Overheight containers can be carried below.
5 Efficiency
Economic carriage and efficient loading and discharging of containers.
Specially designed stacking fittings and pins.
Minimal lashing requirements.
Large hatch covers can be stored on top of small hatch covers for ease of cargo handling.
6 Fast turnaround
Ability to take bunkers at 500 tonnes per hour. Special stores handling facilities.
Bow thruster and four large self tensioning winches allowing rapid mooring and unmooring with minimum crew.
7 Accommodation
First class accommodation throughout with private facilities to most cabins and good recreation areas.
8 Reliability
Specification in accordance with well proved design which has operated successfully for several years.

Technical information

Builder
Hitachi Zosen, Innoshima Shipyard, Japan.
Class
Lloyds Register ✠ 100 A1 ✠ LMC
Regulations
Merchant Shipping Act – Republic of Singapore 1970 and as amended.
Solas 1960 as amended.
International Load Line Convention 1966.
International Regulation for Tonnage Measurement of Vessel.
International Telecommunication Convention 1973 and Radio Regulations 1974.
United States Coast Guard Pollution Prevention from Vessels and Oil Transfer Facilities 1972.
Tonnage
Gross (estimated)   abt. 14,100 GRT
Dimensions
Length overall   abt. 157.00 m
Length between p.p.   145.15 m
Breadth moulded   25.00 m
Depth moulded to 2nd deck 11.15 m
Depth moulded to upper deck 14.02 m
Draft Design   8.00 m
Scantling Draft   9.17 m
Deadweight all told
Max. draft   15430 Tonnes
8 m draft   12000 Tonnes

Speed @ 8.00 m @ 80% mco 18.5 k
Operation range   9000 n. miles
Hatch covers
Precise location of hatch covers allows 10 wide stow on deck with containers stowed across two hatches.
Hatch cover stack loads for 40'0" up to 88 long tons.
Hatch cover stack loads for 20'0" up to 65 long tons.
Tank capacities
Fuel & Diesel oil   1550 m³
Fresh water   110 m³
Ballast water   3720 m³
Accommodation
Officers and Crew: 35
Senior Officers: Suite of Rooms
Officers and Petty Officers: Private Facilities
Crew: Semi Private Facilities
Officers' Dining Room, Lounge and Bar
Crew Dining Room, Lounge and Bar
Caterers' Dining Room, Lounge and Bar
Sundry
4 abt. 15ts. aut. selftension winches (electric).
1 abt. 24ts. windlass (electric).
Bow thruster, 10t thrust, controllable pitch.

Heeling tanks with 500 m³/h pump.
CO₂ fire-fighting system for engine room.
Sewage treatment plant.
Air-conditioned accommodation.
Gyro/auto-pilot – Radio direction finder.
Echo sounder – Two radars – Satellite navigator.
Pilot log – Wireless station – TV/Radio antennas.
Extensive galley equipment.
440/220V, 60 Cycles.
400A shore connection.
80 electric reefer sockets.
Fresh water generator 21 tonnes/day.
Machinery
Main engine Hitachi Sulzer 6RND76 MCR 12000 BHP operable on 1500 sec. Redwood No. 1 at 100°F.
Fixed pitch propeller.
Auxiliary engines, 3 x 500 kw @ 1200 rpm. 3 x 440V, 60 Cycles.
Emergency diesel 250 kw.
Auxiliary boiler 1200 kg/h, 7 kg/cm² saturated.
Exhaust gas economiser 1200 kg/h, 7 kg/cm² saturated.
FO & LO separators of self-cleaning type.
Bilge water separator.

1
Design Firm, **Raymond Bennett Design
Associates, PTY, Ltd.**
Art Director, **Raymond Bennett**
Designer, **Raymond Bennett**
Illustrator, **Raymond Bennett**
Client, **Timur Carriers Limited**
Six colors on white art board

1

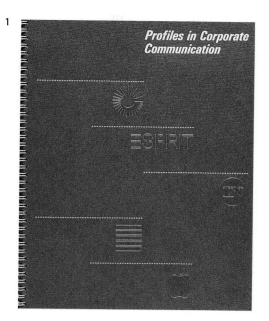

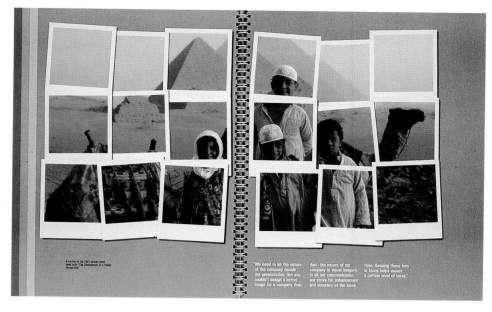

2

1
Design Firm, **Richard Danne & Associates, Inc.**
Art Director, **Richard Danne**
Designer, **Richard Danne/Eric Atherton/**
Margaret Wollenhaupt
Copywriter, **Ralph Caplan**
Client, **The Simpson Paper Co.**
Five colors on Simpson Gainsborough &
Vicksburg Vellum

2
Design Firm, **Handler Group, Inc.**
Art Director, **Mark L. Handler/Tom Dolle**
Designer, **Tom Dolle**
Photographer, **Roger Bester**
Copywriter, **Howard Flashenberg/**
Mark L. Handler/Ed Keller
Client, **ESPN**
Six colors

1
Design Firm, **McCargar Design**
Art Director, **Kyle Ajifu/Morris Advertising &
Design, Inc.**
Designer, **Lucy McCargar**
Photographer, **Jerry Laursen**
Copywriter, **Morris Advertising & Design, Inc.**
Client, **Stevenson Ranch**
Six colors and varnish on Vintage gloss, die-cut on
right side

2
Design Firm, **McCargar Design**
Art Director, **Lucy McCargar/Reid Advertising**
Designer, **Lucy McCargar**
Photographer, **Art Coleman**
Copywriter, **Reid Advertising**
Client, **The J.F. Temple Co.**
Five colors and varnish on Quintessence gloss

1
Design Firm, **Muller & Co.**
Art Director, **Mark Anderson**
Designer, **Mark Anderson**
Photographer, **Ron Berg/Vedros & Associates**
Copywriter, **David Marks**
Client, **DST**
Six colors on Centura gloss

2
Design Firm, **DMCD**
Art Director, **Richard Downes**
Designer, **Tom Neilson**
Photographer, **Rusty Ristine, Inc.**
Copywriter, **Du Pont**
Client, **Du Pont**
Five colors on Reflections cover

1
Design Firm, **Michael Stanard, Inc.**
Art Director, **Michael Stanard**
Designer, **Marcos Chavez**
Photographer, **David Wagenaar**
Client, **Open Court Publishing**

2
Design Firm, **Michael Stanard, Inc.**
Art Director, **Michael Stanard**
Designer, **Lisa Fingerhut**
Photographer, **Uldis Saule**
Client, **Kraft General Foods**
Six colors on Mohawk 50/10

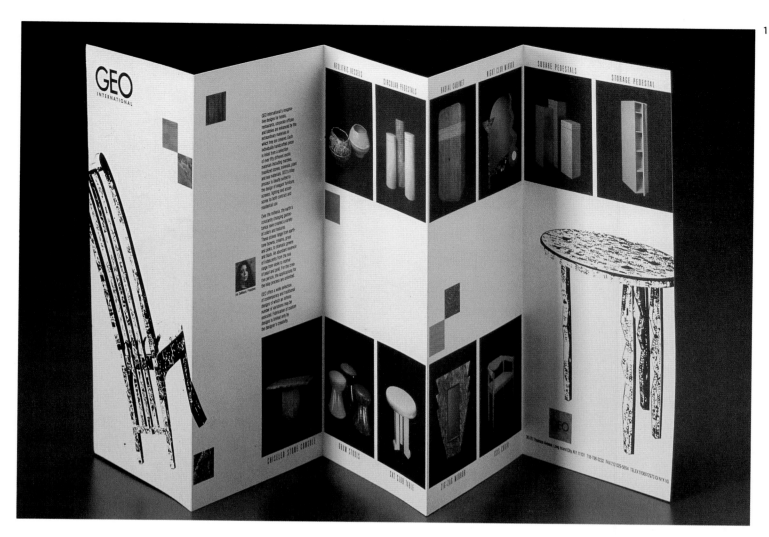

1
Design Firm, **Platinum Design, Inc.**
Art Director, **Vickie Peslak**
Designer, **Vickie Peslak**
Client, **Geo International Furniture**

2
Design Firm, **Clifford Selbert Design**
Art Director, **Clifford Selbert**
Designer, **Melanie Lowe**
Photographer, **Susie Cushner**
Copywriter, **Kim Carlin**
Client, **M Brown**
Five colors

SERVICE BOOKLETS

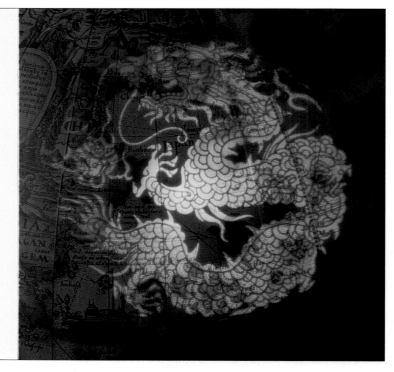

1
Design Firm, **Alan Chan Design Co.**
Art Director, **Alan Chan**
Designer, **Alan Chan/Jensen Choi**
Photographer, **Sandy Lee**
Client, **Megaway Investment Holdings, Ltd.**
Six colors on matte art paper, art card

*A dragon is used as a symbolic element throughout
because it represents strength, power, and status.
The company logo on the cover symbolizes a dragon
over the water.*

THE GUILIN PLAZA

Picturesque Guilin, a popular holiday resort, is China's fourth most important tourist destination.

The 298 — room Guilin Plaza commands a panaramic view of idyllic Guilin.

A joint venture between the Guilin Travel and Tourism Bureau and a wholly owned subsidiary of the Company, this is the Tourism Bureau's first direct participation in a hotel project.

桂林觀光酒店

風光如畫的桂林,一直是旅遊勝地,
是中國第四大旅遊重點。於去年使用。詳
實房二百九十八間的桂林觀光酒店,園即
桂林風光。

這是桂林旅遊局和菲華集團之全資附
屬公司合資桂辦,旅遊局首次參與酒店投
資項目。

TRAVELLERS' BUSINESS CENTRES

The dramatic increase in overseas visitors to China — an average annual rate of almost 25% over the past 12 years — is also reflected in the growth of business travellers to China, most of whom need efficient and readily available business and travel-related services and communication facilities.

Capitalising on it's strong relationship with the Shanghai Railway Bureau, Megaway has undertaken a joint venture agreement with the Railway Bureau to open a network of Travellers' Business Centres in leased locations at railway stations. A chain of Centres is planned, the first in Shanghai — to open by fourth quarter 1991 — a second in Xiamen and subsequently in the five provinces and one city over which the Railway Bureau has jurisdiction.

To meet the business and travel-related service needs of business travellers, the Centres will offer business and telecommunication services and provide room booking, reservation and ticketing services to complement the Company's hotel and travel agency business. Each centre will have a C.L. Thomson desk for overseas bookings.

旅客商務中心

中國海外旅客的迅速增長 —— 過去十
二年平均年增幅近百分之二十五。同樣地
映射出中國差務旅客的增長上。也們大都
台需要有效率的商務及旅遊相關服務及通
訊設施。

建同上海鐵路局的良好關係。菲業集
團同上海鐵路局達成合資經營協議。在車
站的出租地方設立旅客商務中心。設計劃
開設一連串中心。第一間設於上海。於一
九九一年底開辦。第二間在廈門。然後續
在鐵路網絡內五省一市車站內開設。

爲滿足商務旅客的需求。中心將提供
商核及通訊服務。並提供訂房。訂位。訂
票等服務。每一中心並有 C.L. Thomson
服務桌。提供海外訂位服務。

Dynamic growth characterises the rise

of Hong Kong from a bare, rocky island

to an international business centre.

Hutchison Whampoa Limited

Annual Report 1990

The panoramic
photographs that appear in
this report have been
created with a roundabout
camera. Using a swift,
360 degree exposure, this
unique camera captures a
fully circular, distortion-
free perspective.

It is also reflected in the development

of Hutchison Whampoa from a local

trading company to a diversified

international corporation. The Group

has played an important role in

Hong Kong's development. With

its roots firmly planted in the territory,

Hutchison Whampoa is expanding

its perspective with overseas investments.

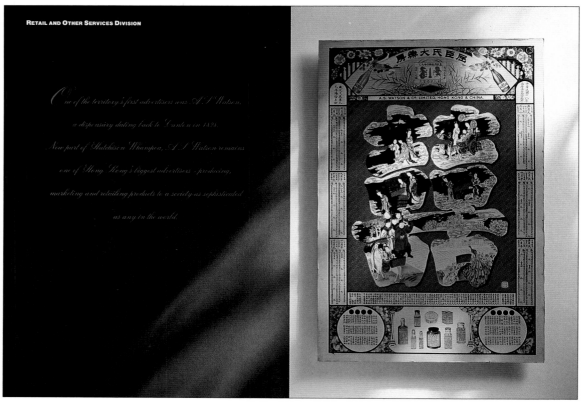

RETAIL AND OTHER SERVICES DIVISION

One of the territory's first advertisers was A.S.Watson,

a dispensary dating back to Canton in 1828.

Now part of Hutchison Whampoa, A.S.Watson remains

one of Hong Kong's biggest advertisers - producing,

marketing and retailing products to a society as sophisticated

as any in the world.

1
Design Firm, **Alan Chan Design Co.**
Art Director, **Alan Chan**
Designer, **Alan Chan/Cetric Leung**
Photographer, **Raymond Wong/Stock Photo**
Copywriter, **Hill and Knowlton**
Client, **Hutchison Whampoa Ltd.**
Six colors on matte paper, art card

The Group operates 57 Watson's personal care stores in Hong Kong, which benefit from increased consumer sophistication and spending power.

*P*rofit before extraordinary items was HK$396 million (1989 — HK$448 million). The decrease in profit contribution is mainly due to the disposal of trading and engineering subsidiaries John D. Hutchison Group Limited and Hutchison-Boag Engineering Limited at the start of 1990. In addition, the increased profits generated by the Hong Kong operations of Park'N Shop, Watson's and the Telecommunications group were partially offset by the costs associated with the expansion of their overseas operations which are in various stages of development.

The Group's retail operations continued to expand into the region, introducing new products and innovative store technology to a wider market place.

A.S. WATSON & COMPANY LIMITED
In a successful year of operations, A S Watson accelerated its strategy for regional expansion, while achieving increased profitability from existing retail and manufacturing operations.

Continued investment in the Park'N Shop supermarket chain saw 10 new stores opened in Hong Kong, bringing the territory's total to 140 shops by year end. Installation of a branch computing system enhanced the chain's reputation for store innovation. A HK$200 million fresh food depot being developed at Sheung Shui in the New Territories is set for completion in mid-1991.

Park'N Shop's overseas expansion continued with the opening of nine new stores in Taiwan and two stores in both Thailand and China. As these stores are still in their early stages of operation, they are unlikely to make a meaningful contribution in the short term.

During a year of successful profit development, Watson's personal care stores withstood the combined difficulties of reduced consumer spending, a weaker tourist market and high rent increases. Four more stores were opened in Hong Kong.

Watson's is one of Asia's best known retail concepts and that recognition is growing. A further nine stores were opened overseas, and a second store in China was opened in Shanghai in early 1991. The Watson's chain now totals 96 outlets in Hong Kong, Macau, Taiwan, Singapore and China.

Retail, Telecommunications and Other Services Turnover
(HK$ millions)
☐ Overseas
■ Hong Kong

24

25

No city on earth matches Hong Kong's demand for portable phones. Hutchison serves this market with state-of-the-art technology and innovative marketing. Now the Group is expanding this service in other markets overseas.

*W*ide-ranging expansion into Asia and Europe highlighted the Telecommunications group's growing prominence among the world's mobile communication service providers. With the development of new operations in Thailand, Taiwan, Malaysia and Bangladesh, further investment in Australia and the UK, and continued leadership of the Hong Kong mobile communications market, Hutchison Telecom continued its pattern of strong growth.

Cellular Telephone Subscribers
Hong Kong and United Kingdom

HONG KONG OPERATIONS
Consistently the market leader in Hong Kong's paging market, Hutchison Paging added a further 50,000 subscribers during 1990, with innovative products such as the financial news pager being introduced during the year. Hutchison Paging also applied successfully for a licence to operate Hong Kong's second generation cordless telephone system (CT2). Construction of the system is set to commence during 1991.

Excellent growth was enjoyed by Hutchison Telephone which — with 67,000 subscribers — supplies over 55% of Hong Kong's cellular telephone services. To complement its cellular service, Hutchison Telephone also introduced Hong Kong's first 800Mhz 2-way trunked radio service.

Hutchison Mobile Data launched its innovative wireless modem during 1990 while iNet Hong Kong — which provides sophisticated network-based information services — grew steadily during the year.

Metro Broadcast, in which the Group holds a 29% interest, was awarded the licence in December 1990 to run Hong Kong's second commercial radio station. Operations are expected to commence in mid-1991.

ASIA PACIFIC OPERATIONS
Hutchison Telecommunications Australia, now a 70% owned subsidiary, is already a significant player in Australia with an expanding paging network which serves over 50,000 subscribers in five states.

Operations of a nationwide paging network in Thailand, in which the Group has a 45% interest, commenced late in the year. The Group also entered into a joint venture agreement to provide secretarial paging services in Taiwan. Expansion into Malaysia was achieved through the acquisition of a 28.5% interest in a national paging licence. Additionally, a joint venture to supply cellular services to Bangladesh is expected to start operations during 1991.

EUROPEAN OPERATIONS
Already one of the UK's top four cellular service providers, Hutchison Telecommunications UK strengthened its operations in Britain through the acquisition of Nokia Mobira, a cellular service provider with 25,000 subscribers.

30

31

1
Design Firm, **Bernhardt Fudyma Design Group**
Art Director, **Craig Bernhardt/Janice Fudyma**
Designer, **Carol Melloni**
Client, **Kidder Peabody**
Four process colors/two PMS colors

The cover is embossed and stamped.

2
Design Firm, **Bernhardt Fudyma Design Group**
Art Director, **Craig Bernhardt/Janice Fudyma**
Designer, **Jane Sobczak**
Illustrator, **Richard Hess**
Copywriter, **Stan Hironaka**
Client, **Citicorp**
Four process colors/one PMS color

1
Design Firm, **Bernhardt Fudyma Design Group**
Art Director, **Craig Bernhardt/Janice Fudyma**
Designer, **Janice Fudyma**
Illustrator, **Kinuko Craft**
Copywriter, **Stan Hironaka**
Client, **Citicorp**
Four process colors/one PMS color

2
Design Firm, **Bernhardt Fudyma Design Group**
Art Director, **Craig Bernhardt/Janice Fudyma**
Designer, **Iris Brown/Janice Fudyma**
Photographer, **Lynn Sugarman**
Client, **Kidder Peabody**
Four process colors/one PMS color, tinted varnish

1

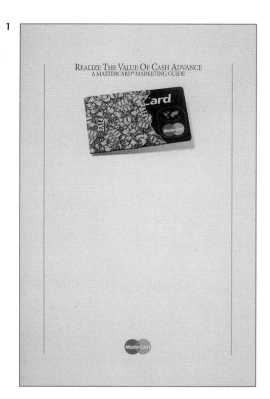

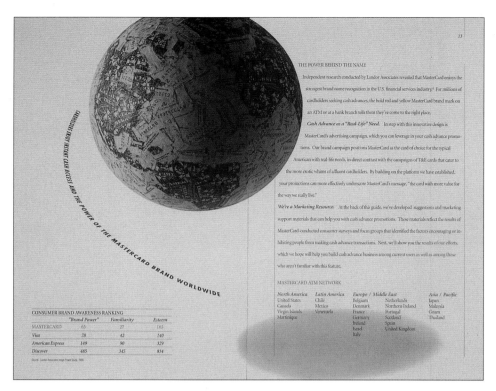

2

1
Design Firm, **Bernhardt Fudyma Design Group**
Art Director, **Craig Bernhardt/Janice Fudyma**
Designer, **Iris Brown**
Currency Sculptor, **Barton Benes**
Photographer, **Earl Ripling**
Client, **Master Card**
Four process colors/two PMS colors on Simpson
Starwhite Vicksburg Tiara, High-Tech finish

2
Design Firm, **Bernhardt Fudyma Design Group**
Art Director, **Craig Bernhardt/Janice Fudyma**
Designer, **Iris Brown**
Origami Master, **Michael Shall**
Photographer, **Richard Levy**
Client, **Citibank**
Four process colors/two PMS colors on Hopper
Tapestry Silk

1
Design Firm, **Adele Bass & Co. Design**
Art Director, **Adele Bass**
Designer, **Adele Bass**
Photographer, **Rob Outwater**
Copywriter, **Sharynn Bass**
Client, **Rockwell Federal Credit Union**
Four colors and spot varnish

2
Design Firm, **Adele Bass & Co. Design**
Art Director, **Adele Bass**
Designer, **Adele Bass**
Photographer, **Rob Outwater**
Copywriter, **Starr Kelley**
Client, **Rockwell Federal Credit Union**
Five colors on 80-lb. Quintessence dull cover

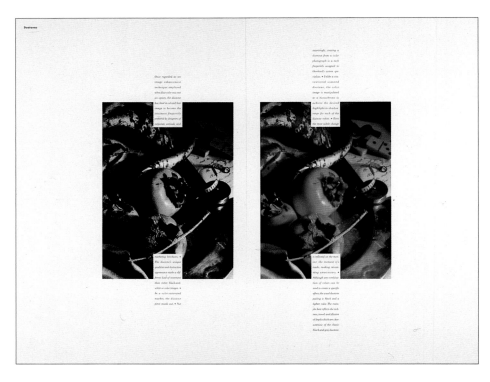

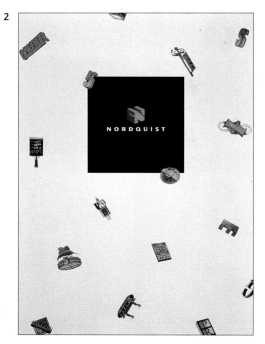

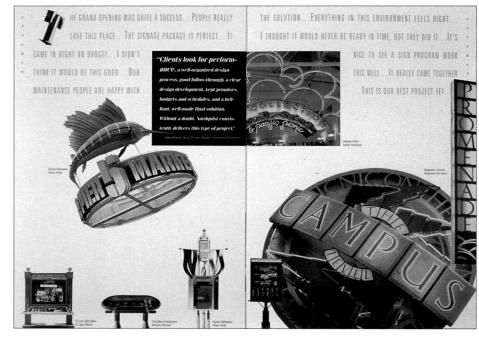

1
Design Firm, **Besser Joseph Partners**
Art Director, **Douglas Joseph/Rik Besser**
Designer, **Douglas Joseph**
Photographer, **Michele Clement**
Copywriter, **Overland Printers**
Client, **Overland Printers**
Six colors on Reflections

2
Design Firm, **Communication Arts, Inc.**
Art Director, **Richard Foy/David A. Shelton**
Designer, **Dave Tweed**
Copywriter, **Communication Arts, Inc.**
Client, **Nordquist Sign Co.**
Four colors and spot lamination on Quintessence

Design Firm, **Morris/Beecher, Inc.**
Art Director, **Diane Beecher**
Designer, **Diane Beecher**
Copywriter, **Mark Morris**
Client, **Lord Associates**
Six colors on Lustro dull Cream

*The client requested a corporate brochure that broke
the norm of traditional brochures, one that would
leave a lasting impression. We created a binding and
die-cut method after five printers said a perfectly
round brochure with no straight edges was
impossible.*

1
Design Firm, **Morris/Beecher, Inc.**
Art Director, **Diane Beecher**
Designer, **Diane Beecher**
Photographer, **Ross Chappel/Ron Starr/**
Mark Segal
Copywriter, **Mark Morris**
Client, **McArthur/Glen**
Six colors

2
Design Firm, **O & J Design, Inc.**
Art Director, **Andrzej Olejniczak**
Designer, **Andrzej Olejniczak**
Illustrator, **Andrzej Dudzinski**
Copywriter, **Steve Rothman**
Client, **Sotheby's**
Five colors

1
Design Firm, **Ascent Communications**
Art Director, **Allen Haeger**
Designer, **Allen Haeger**
Photographer, **Orin Yost**
Copywriter, **Carolyn Yost**
Client, **FEI**
Four process colors/one metallic color

2
Design Firm, **Smith Art Direction and
Design Associates**
Art Director, **James Smith**
Designer, **John Korinko/James Smith**
Illustrator, **Joe Milioto**
Photographer, **Vic Tartaglia**
Copywriter, **John Turi**
Client, **Colonial Graphics**
Four process colors/one PMS color, one gloss/one
dull varnish on 85-lb. Reflection gloss cover

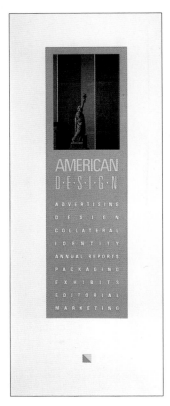

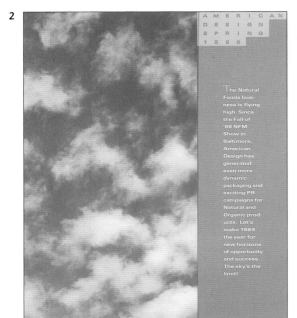

1
Design Firm, **Ascent Communications**
Art Director, **Allen Haeger**
Designer, **Allen Haeger**
Photographer, **David Sharpe**
Copywriter, **Susan Haeger**
Client, **American Design**
Four process colors

2
Design Firm, **Ascent Communications**
Art Director, **Allen Haeger**
Designer, **Allen Haeger**
Photographer, **David Sharpe**
Copywriter, **Susan Haeger**
Client, **American Design**
Four process colors/one special-mix green

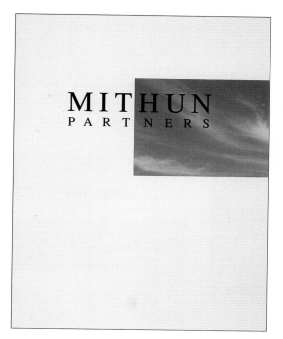
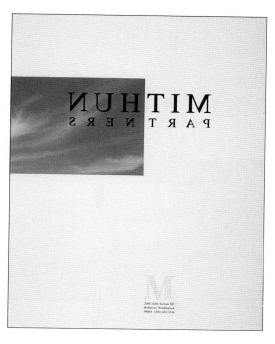

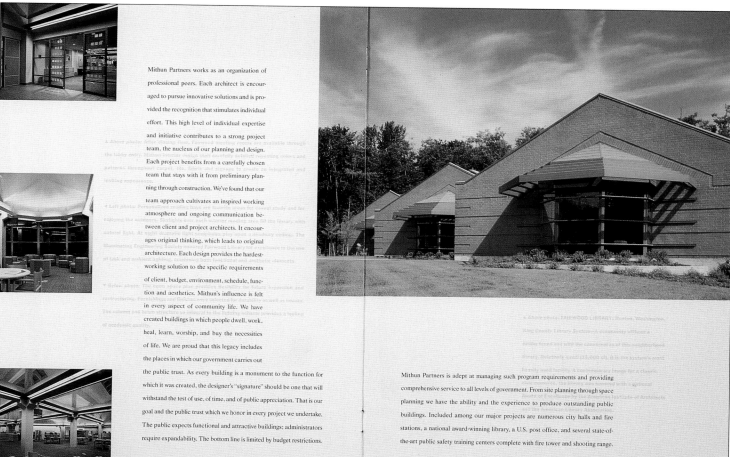

1
Design Firm, **Art Chantry Design**
Art Director, **Art Chantry**
Designer, **Art Chantry**
Copywriter, **Mithun Partners**
Client, **Mithun Partners**
Four process colors, and one varnish on coated
matte

*Through various mirror-image design references, this
brochure evokes the architectural style of this group.*

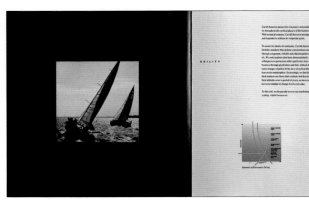

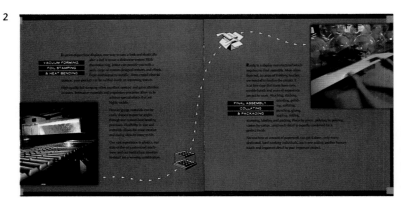

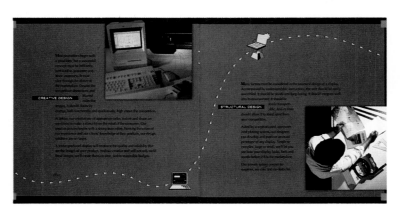

1

Design Firm, **Donovan and Green**
Art Director, **Nancye Green/Julie Riefler**
Designer, **Julie Riefler**
Photographer, **Rodney Smith**
Copywriter, **Torrance & Associates**
Client, **Carvill America**
Four process colors, two varnishes on
Ikonolux gloss

2

Design Firm, **Notovitz Design, Inc.**
Art Director, **Joseph Notovitz/Gil Livne**
Designer, **Gil Livne**
Illustrator, **Gil Livne/Jack Suzuky**
Photographer, **Roy Silverstein**
Copywriter, **Joseph Notovitz**
Client, **Jomar Displays**
Eight colors on Mead Signature

*This booklet was created entirely on the Mac
(excluding the photos which were separated
traditionally to maintain the highest possible quality)
and was output on RC paper with a Linotronic
Imagesetter.*

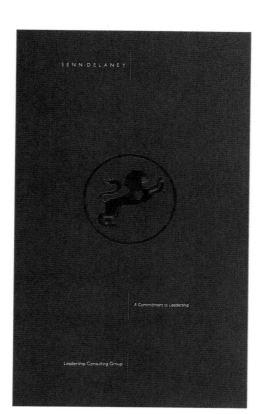

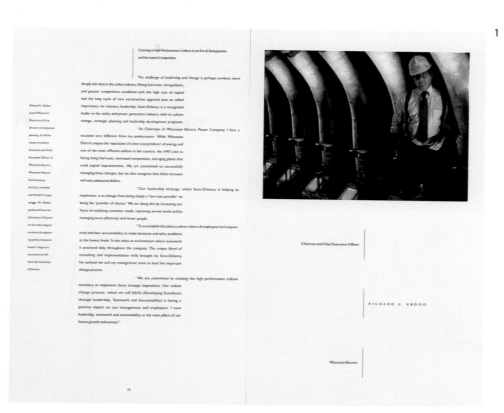

1
Design Firm, **Besser Joseph Partners**
Art Director, **Douglas Joseph/Rik Besser**
Designer, **Douglas Joseph**
Photographer, **Neil Slavin**
Copywriter, **Senn-Delaney**
Client, **Senn-Delaney**
Six colors on Reflections Teton

2
Design Firm, **Herbst LaZar Bell, Inc./
Spek'trem Division**
Art Director, **Robert Lavin**
Designer, **Pamela Anderson**
Photographer, **Charles Johnson**
Copywriter, **Kim Visokie**
Client, **JBS & Associates**
Eight colors on 100-lb. Quintessence

This brochure design integrates an interesting combination of paper types and visuals, creating an exciting visual piece that enhances the communication of the firm's target message.

1

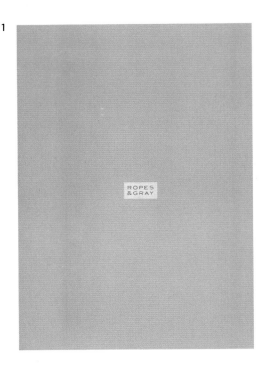

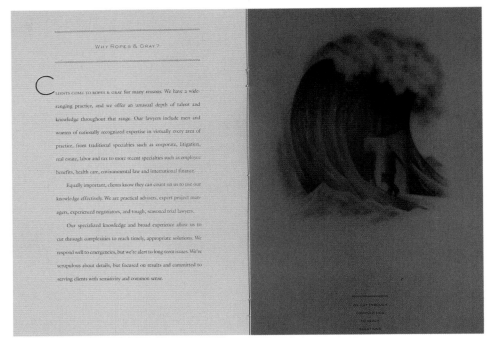

2

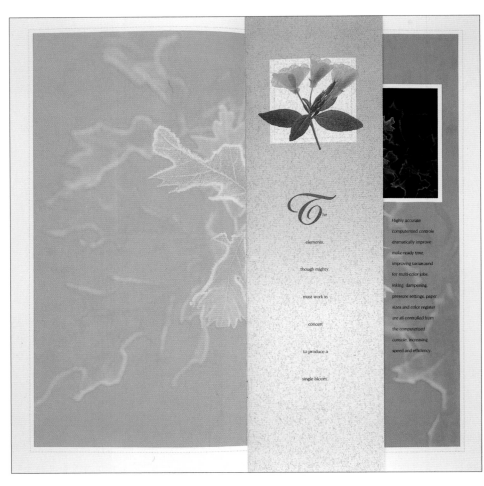

1
Design Firm, **Tyler Smith**
Art Director, **Tyler Smith**
Designer, **Tyler Smith**
Illustrator, **Fred Lynch**
Copywriter, **John Temple**
Client, **Ropes & Gray**
Fourteen colors on Warren Cameo

This prestigious Boston-based law firm brochure incorporates understated, classic design with monochromatic illustrations.

2
Design Firm, **Myklebust Brockman, Inc.**
Art Director, **Stephanie Fraase Severson**
Designer, **Stephanie Fraase Severson**
Illustrator, **Stephanie Fraase Severson**
Photographer, **Jon Walton/Third Eye Photography and Dick Swift/AVS, Inc.**
Copywriter, **Elly S. Hopkins**
Client, **La Crosse Graphics, Inc.**
Six colors, two varnishes on Evergreen &
Remarque White gloss

Printed with organic oil-based inks on recycled paper.

Communication is integral to problem solving.

We begin by listening. And through each stage of production, we emphasize a level of communication which encourages creative and cost-effective solutions. Your priorities are addressed, from press proofing and scheduling to your concern for environmentally responsible choices.

We've responded with a wider variety of recycled stocks. Soybean-based inks are used extensively on our new Mitsubishi press, with unparalleled sharpness and clarity. Our dampening systems are now alcohol-free, eliminating the release of noxious fumes into the atmosphere and creating a more healthful work environment.

1

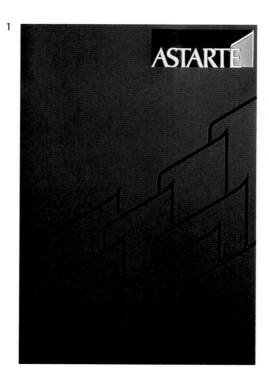

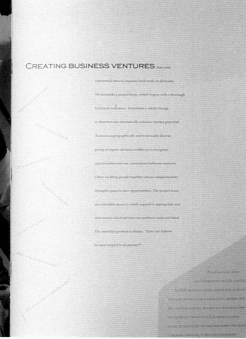

CREATING BUSINESS VENTURES that yield

2

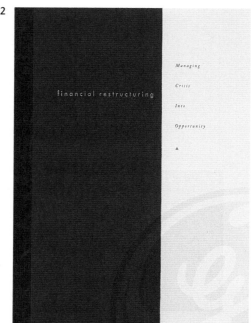
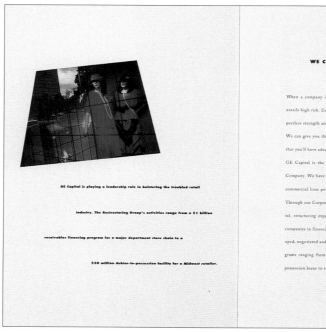

WE CAN SWING THE MOMENTUM

IN YOUR FAVOR

When a company is in financial distress, every management decision entails high risk. Except for the selection of a financial partner with the peerless strength and expertise of GE Capital. *Forward momentum* ▸ We can give you the power to turn things around. Plus the confidence that you'll have adequate capital to keep your company moving forward. GE Capital is the principal financial subsidiary of General Electric Company. We have more than $70 billion in assets and the largest U.S. commercial loan portfolio of any bank or non-bank finance company. Through our Corporate Finance Restructuring Group, we provide capital, structuring expertise and related services to operationally strong companies in financial distress. Over the past two decades, we've developed, negotiated and executed sophisticated financial restructuring programs ranging from recapitalizations to asset purchases to debtor-in-possession loans to receivables securitization programs.

1
Design Firm, **Communication Arts, Inc.**
Art Director, **Richard Foy/David A. Shelton**
Designer, **Dave Tweed**
Photographer, **Thomas Arledge**
Copywriter, **Ginny Hoyle**
Client, **Astarte, Inc.**
Eight colors on Rhododendron 80-lb. cover, Karma 65-lb. cover

This piece features three foils, engraving, and five duotones printed on dry trap pearl varnish.

2
Design Firm, **Wiggin Design, Inc.**
Art Director, **Gail Wiggin**
Designer, **Gail Wiggin**
Photographer, **Stock: Westlight**
Copywriter, **General Electric Capital**
Client, **General Electric Capital**
Five colors, one varnish on Gainsborough Hunter Green 80-lb. cover, Trophy 52-lb. gloss cover text

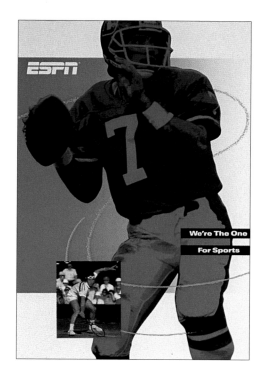

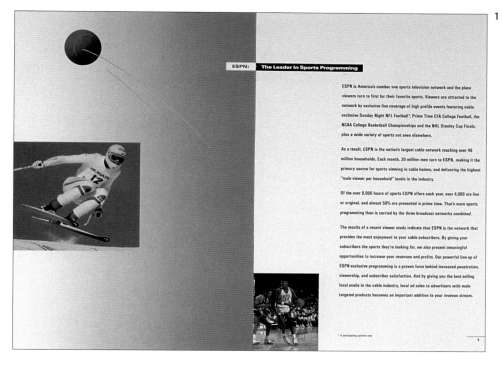

1
Design Firm, **Handler Group, Inc.**
Art Director, **Mark L. Handler**
Designer, **Tom Dolle/Paul Biederman**
Copywriter, **Howard Flashenberg/**
Mark L. Handler
Client, **ESPN**
Eight colors, one matte/one gloss varnish

2
Design Firm, **Handler Group, Inc.**
Art Director, **Mark L. Handler**
Designer, **Tom Dolle/Debra Gassner**
Copywriter, **Howard Flashenberg**
Client, **ESPN**
Eight colors/two varnishes

1
Design Firm, **Handler Group, Inc.**
Art Director, **Mark L. Handler**
Designer, **Tom Dolle**
Copywriter, **Howard Flashenberg/**
Mark L. Handler
Client, **ESPN**

2
Design Firm, **The Weller Institute for the Cure**
of Design, Inc.
Art Director, **Don Weller**
Designer, **Don Weller**
Illustrator, **Don Weller**
Photographer, **Michael Schoenfeld**
Client, **Industrial Design Associates**
Four process colors/four match colors and varnish
on Cameo, Kromekote, and Mylar

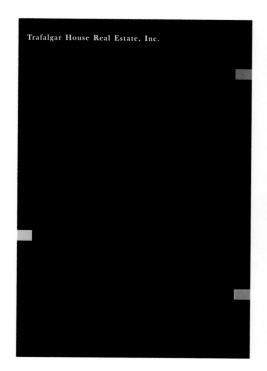

Trafalgar House Real Estate, Inc.

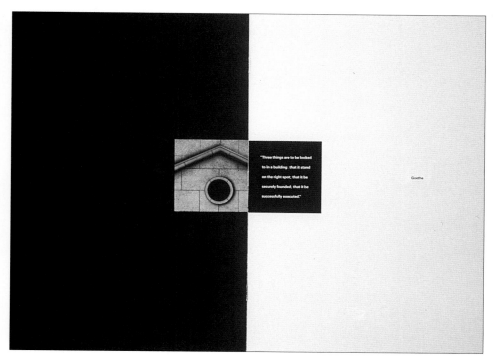

"These things are to be looked to in a building: that it stand on the right spot; that it be securely founded; that it be successfully executed."

Goethe

CONSTRUCTION MANAGEMENT

"The rapid development of technology and communications necessitates ongoing reassessment of the built environment."

John L. W. Foot
Construction

*200 Greenwich Avenue
Greenwich, Connecticut
Mixed use—retail and
office with parking garage
100,000 square feet*

*Thorndal
Darien, Connecticut
Office development
30,000 square feet*

From the very start of a project, the Construction Management Group works in close cooperation with the Planning, Design and Marketing Groups. In this way we make certain that every new development complies with the statutory approvals and consents, and thoroughly satisfies potential tenant needs—from dust-free environments to acoustical installations.

Schedules and costs are regularly checked to ensure that target completion dates are met. We analyze designs; oversee building systems; monitor the selection of materials, highway and off-site improvements; and maintain strict control over budgets and

schedules, as well as the bidding and administration of individual trade contracts.

Over the years, the Company has built high-rise condominiums, office buildings, corporate parks, mixed-use and specialized buildings.

Drawing on this experience and that afforded by the worldwide activities of Trafalgar House, we can tell how best to build a particular project, the most efficient way to manage it, who to call and the hard questions to ask. And when the building is complete, our presence continues in a full range of management services.

*David J. Stasse
Project Manager*

*Ralph W. Beyer
Vice President, Construction*

IX

1
Design Firm, **Donovan and Green**
Art Director, **Nancye Green/Julie Riefler**
Designer, **Julie Riefler**
Photographer, **Gregory Heisler**
Client, **Trafalgar House Real Estate, Inc.**
Five colors, two varnishes on Consolidated

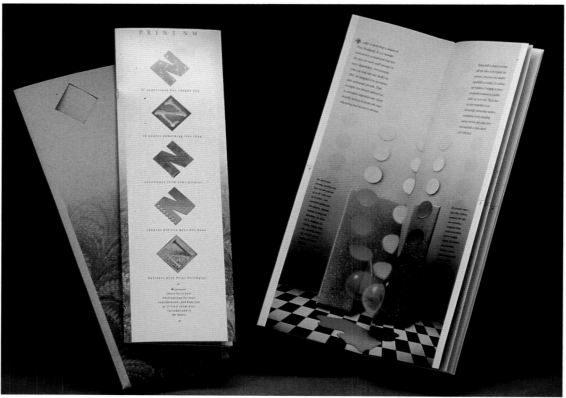

1
Design Firm, **Hornall Anderson Design Works**
Art Director, **Jack Anderson**
Designer, **Jack Anderson/Heidi Hatlestad/**
Jani Drewfs
Copywriter, **Fran Olson**
Client, **Print Northwest**
12 colors, varnish, and foil stamping on Lustro dull
cover, Sleeve - Gainsborough

1
Design Firm, **Hornall Anderson Design Works**
Art Director, **Julia LaPine**
Designer, **Julia LaPine/Heidi Hatlestad/Lian Ng**
Illustrator, **Javier Romero Design**
Photographer, **Jeff Zarbuba**
Copywriter, **John Koval**
Client, **Airborne Express**
Nine colors on Lustro gloss

2
Design Firm, **Hornall Anderson Design Works**
Art Director, **John Hornall**
Designer, **John Hornall/Paula Cox**
Copywriter, **Sam Angeloff**
Client, **Muzak Corp.**
Eight colors on Vintage

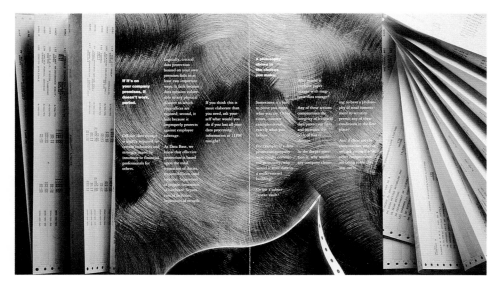
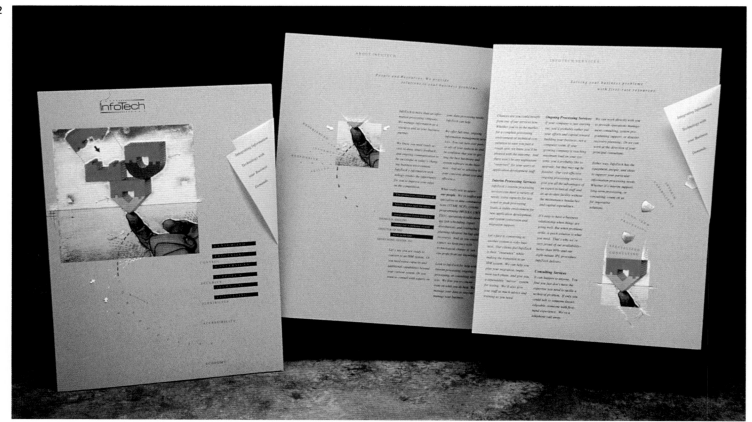

1
Design Firm, **Hornall Anderson Design Works**
Art Director, **Luann Bice**
Designer, **Luann Bice/Julie Tanagi-Lock/**
Brian O'Neill
Illustrator, **David Lesh**
Copywriter, **InfoTech Corp.**
Client, **InfoTech Corp.**
Four process colors/two PMS colors, and varnish

2
Design Firm, **Hornall Anderson Design Works**
Art Director, **John Hornall**
Designer, **John Hornall/Denise Weir**
Photographer, **Kevin Latona**
Copywriter, **Christiansen & Fritsch**
Client, **Data Base**
Six colors on Ikonolux

1
Design Firm, **Hornall Anderson Design Works**
Art Director, **Jack Anderson**
Designer, **Jack Anderson/David Bates**
Illustrator, **Gary Eldridge**
Copywriter, **Bill Rozier**
Client, **Services Group of America**
Six colors on Starwhite Vicksburg

2
Design Firm, **Hornall Anderson Design Works**
Art Director, **Jack Anderson**
Designer, **Jack Anderson/Julie Tanagi-Lock/Lian Ng**
Copywriter, **Bill Rozier**
Client, **Services Group of America**
Five colors on LOE

1
Design Firm, **Hornall Anderson Design Works**
Art Director, **Jack Anderson**
Designer, **Jack Anderson/David Bates/
Leo Raymundo**
Photographer, **Tom Collicott**
Copywriter, **Pamela Mason-Davey**
Client, **Services Group of America**
Seven colors on Ikonolux dull

2
Design Firm, **Hornall Anderson Design Works**
Art Director, **Jack Anderson/Luann Bice**
Designer, **Luann Bice/Debra Shishkoff/
Paula Cox/Jack Anderson**
Illustrator, **Jerry Nelson**
Copywriter, **Williams, Zografos & Peck**
Client, **Williams, Zografos & Peck**
Two colors on Passport

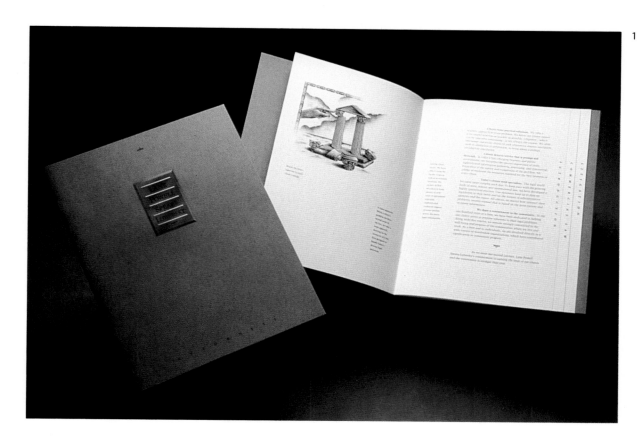

1
Design Firm, **Hornall Anderson Design Works**
Art Director, **Jack Anderson**
Designer, **Jack Anderson/Mary Hermes**
Illustrator, **Jonathan Combs**
Copywriter, **Robin Anderson**
Client, **Lane Powell Spears Lubersky**
Six colors on Paloma matte

2
Design Firm, **Hornall Anderson Design Works**
Art Director, **John Hornall**
Designer, **John Hornall/Denise Weir**
Illustrator, **John Hornall/Denise Weir/**
Heidi Hatlestad
Photographer, **Robin Bartholick/Steve Kaiser**
Copywriter, **Sam Angeloff**
Client, **Intermec Corp.**
Six colors on Gainsborough Brilliant Art gloss

1

2

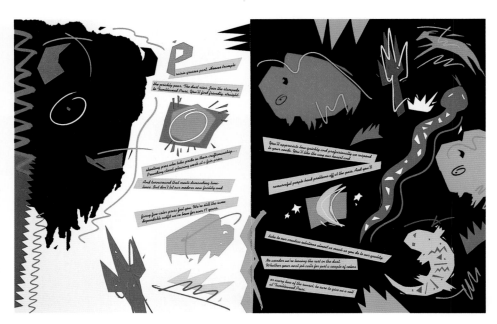

1
Design Firm, **Lee Reedy Design Associates, Inc.**
Art Director, **Lee Reedy**
Designer, **Lee Reedy**
Illustrator, **Mathew McFarren**
Photographer, **Ron Coppock**
Copywriter, **Ginny Hoyle**
Client, **Tumbleweed Press**
Ten colors and varnish on LOE

2
Design Firm, **Lee Reedy Design Associates, Inc.**
Art Director, **Lee Reedy**
Designer, **Lee Reedy**
Illustrator, **Lee Reedy/Heather Bartlett/**
Jerry Simpson (cover art)
Photographer, **Roger Reynolds**
Client, **Tumbleweed Press**
Nine colors on LOE

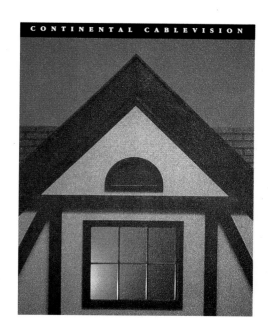

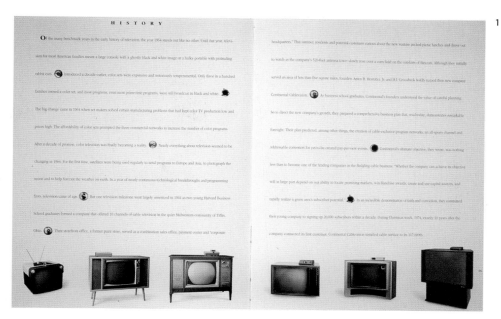

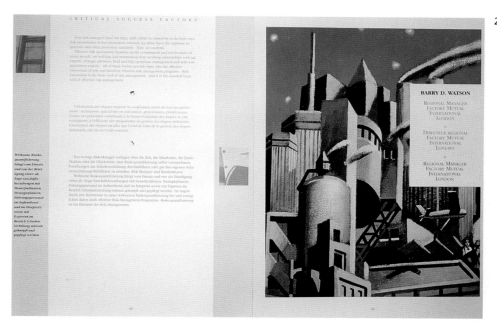

1
Design Firm, **Cordella Design, Inc.**
Art Director, **Andreé Cordella**
Designer, **Andreé Cordella**
Photographer, **Lou Jones**
Copywriter, **Henry James**
Client, **Continental Cablevision**
Seven colors on Ikonolux by Zanders

2
Design Firm, **Cordella Design, Inc.**
Art Director, **Andreé Cordella**
Designer, **Andreé Cordella**
Copywriter, **various**
Client, **Arkwright Mutual Insurance, Co.**
Eight colors on reflections (divider pages) and
Vicksburg Star White (text pages)

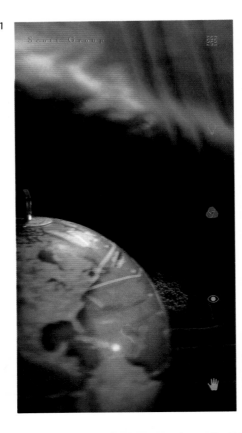

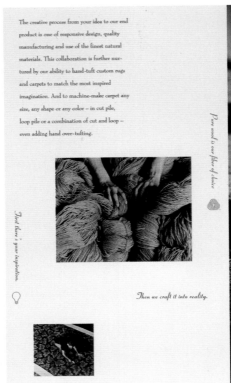

1
Design Firm, **Nesnadny & Schwartz**
Art Director, **Joyce Nesnadny/Mark Schwartz**
Designer, **Joyce Nesnadny**
Photographer, **Vander Lende/
Nesnadny & Schwartz**
Copywriter, **Candace McKinley**
Client, **The Scott Group**
Eight colors on Warren Cameo

2
Design Firm, **Integrate, Inc.**
Art Director, **John Galvin**
Designer, **Steve Quinn/John Galvin**
Photographer, **Larry Friar/Will Shively**
Copywriter, **Lauren Smith**
Client, **Design Central**
Six colors and varnish on Reflections 80-lb. and
100-lb. cover

Large, fold-out images and smaller black-and-white images were shot using high-contrast 35mm Polaroid on-site. The images were then reproduced as duotones with black and metallic silver, with a dull varnish on the black plate.

1
Design Firm, **Pangborn Design, Ltd.**
Art Director, **Dominic Pangborn**
Designer, **Dominic Pangborn**
Illustrator, **Han-Eung Kim**
Photographer, **PHM Corporation**
Copywriter, **PHM Corporation**
Client, **PHM Corporation**
Four process colors/two PMS colors on 85-lb.
Eloquence cover; one color on 3-pt. T2000
(clear sheet)

The cover is laser die-cut.

2
Design Firm, **Pangborn Design, Ltd.**
Art Director, **Dominic Pangborn**
Designer, **Dominic Pangborn/Laura Mysliwiec**
Copywriter, **Russell Gibson von Dohlen**
Client, **Russell Gibson von Dohlen**
Special-mix red, one PMS, spot varnish and
embossing on 111-lb. Ikonolux gloss cover, 74-lb.
Ikonolux gloss text, and 17-lb. UV Ultra

1

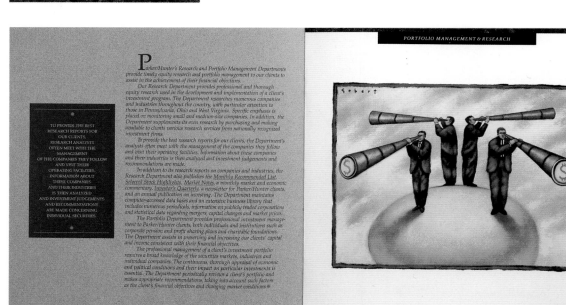

1
Design Firm, **Gray Baumgarten Layport**
Art Director, **Kathy Grubb**
Designer, **Kathy Grubb**
Photographer, **Tom Gigliotto**
Copywriter, **Geoff Tolley**
Client, **Marshall Marketing, Inc.**

2
Design Firm, **Gray Baumgarten Layport**
Art Director, **Kathy Grubb**
Designer, **Kathy Grubb**
Illustrator, **Warren Gerbert**
Copywriter, **Parker/Hunter, Inc.**
Client, **Parker/Hunter, Inc.**
Six colors on Curtis Flannel and Kromekote

1
Design Firm, **Muller & Co.**
Art Director, **John Muller**
Designer, **Scott Chapman**
Photographer, **Mike Regnier**
Copywriter, **David Marks**
Client, **North Kansas City Hospital**
Five colors on Patina matte

2
Design Firm, **Hafeman Design Group**
Art Director, **William Hafeman**
Designer, **William Hafeman/Gabrielle Schubart**
Photographer, **Art Wise**
Copywriter, **Max Russell**
Client, **Warzyn, Inc.**
Four colors

*This pull-tab card (2) geographically announces a
new Air Quality Services capability.*

1
Design Firm, **Pinkhaus Design Corp.**
Art Director, **Joel Fuller**
Designer, **Lisa Ashworth**
Photographer, **Michael Dakota**
Copywriter, **Frank Cunningham**
Client, **Steve Miller/Rex Three, Inc.**
Four match colors on Consolidated Reflections

*"Ghost" images of dogs are printed intentionally on
back pages.*

1
Design Firm, **WRK Design**
Art Director, **Phyllis Pease/Ann Willoughby**
Designer, **Phyllis Pease/Ann Willoughby**
Photographer, **Hollis Officer**
Copywriter, **Anne Simmons**
Client, **Robyn Nichols**
Three colors on Lustre Offset

2
Design Firm, **Richardson or Richardson**
Art Director, **Forrest Richardson**
Designer, **Debi Young Mees**
Photographer, **Rick Gayle/The Gayle Studio**
Client, **The Gayle Studio**
Four process colors

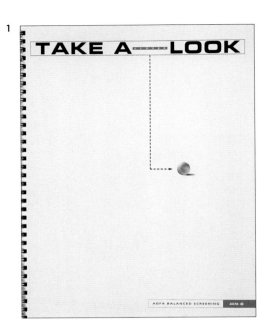

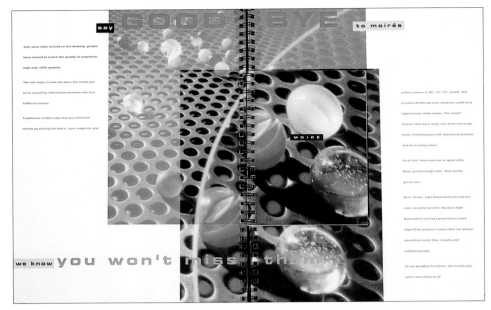

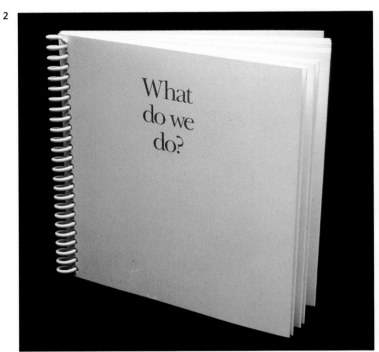

1
Design Firm, **Clifford Selbert Design**
Art Director, **Clifford Selber/Lynn Riddle Waller**
Designer, **Stephanie Wade/Lynn Riddle Waller**
Photographer, **Susie Cushner**
Copywriter, **Kate Thompson**
Client, **Agfa Compugraphics**
Four process colors/one PMS color, S.G.V. on
Consort Royal Silk

2
Design Firm, **Richardson or Richardson**
Art Director, **Valerie Richardson**
Designer, **Valerie Richardson**
Copywriter, **Valerie Richardson**
Client, **Brodsky Associates**
Four process colors

1
Design Firm, **The Bradford Lawton Design Group**
Art Director, **Bradford Lawton/David Halkney/Ellen Pullen**
Designer, **Bradford Lawton/David Halkney**
Photographer, **Swain Edens/Kim Dorroh/David Langford**
Copywriter, **Kim Dorroh**
Client, **CDH**
Four process colors/two PMS colors

1
Design Firm, **Emery/Poe Design**
Art Director, **David Poe**
Designer, **David Poe**
Photographer, **Tony Stone Worldwide**
Copywriter, **Michael Collins**
Client, **Alexander Industries Corp.**
Four process colors/two PMS metallic colors and
varnish on Quintessence gloss cover

2
Design Firm, **Emery/Poe Design**
Art Director, **David Poe**
Designer, **David Poe/Jonathan Mulcare**
Photographer, **Allan Krosnick**
Copywriter, **Michael Collins**
Client, **Feldman, Waldman & Kline Law Firm**
Four process colors/two PMS colors and varnish on
Curtis Gradations, Karma cover and
Curtis Parchkin

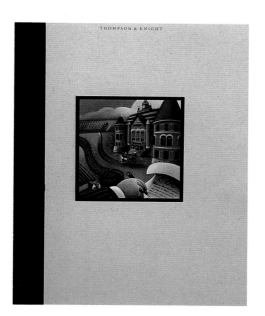

1
Design Firm, **Dennard Creative, Inc.**
Art Director, **Bob Dennard**
Designer, **Bob Dennard/Chuck Johnson**
Illustrator, **Terry Widner**
Photographer, **Jim Olvera**
Copywriter, **Elizabeth Simpson**
Client, **Thompson & Knight**
Four colors on LOE

8+1

Eight Colors and Coating in One Pass

Sandy Alexander has installed the first eight color sheet-fed press with a coater to afford more flexibility with color and design.

Imagine running combinations of process color, match colors and spot varnishes or overall water-based coatings all in one pass. No more gritty powder... no more register problems... and no more ghosting.

You create it and we will do the rest.

For more information on our 8-color press and our **Guide to Color Selection** fill in and return the enclosed reply card.

Sandy Alexander Inc. can do it now!
Web & Sheetfed Lithography.
200 Entin Road, Clifton, NJ 07014   (201) 470-8100   (212) 765-3035

1
Design Firm, **George Tscherny, Inc.**
Art Director, **George Tscherny**
Designer, **George Tscherny**
Illustrator, **George Tscherny**
Client, **Sandy Alexander, Inc.**
Eight colors on Potlatch Vintage gloss

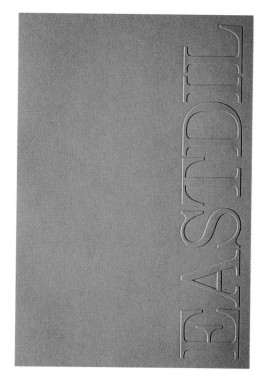

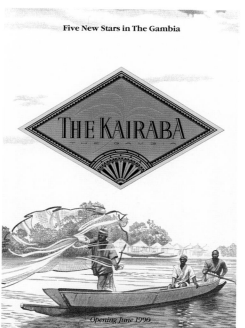

Five New Stars in The Gambia

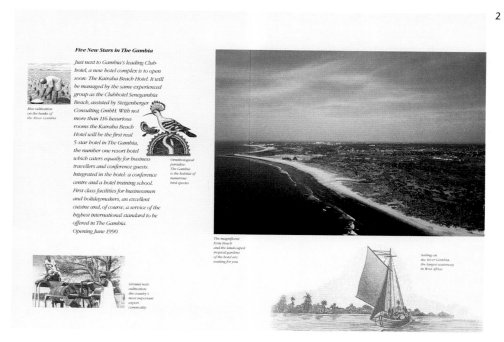

Five New Stars in The Gambia

Just next to Gambia's leading Club-hotel, a new hotel complex is to open soon: The Kairaba Beach Hotel. It will be managed by the same experienced group as the Clubhotel Senegambia Beach, assisted by Steigenberger Consulting GmbH. With not more than 116 luxurious rooms the Kairaba Beach Hotel will be the first real 5-star hotel in The Gambia, the number one resort hotel which caters equally for business travellers and conference guests. Integrated in the hotel: a conference centre and a hotel training school. First class facilities for businessmen and holidaymakers, an excellent cuisine and, of course, a service of the highest international standard to be offered in The Gambia. Opening June 1990.

1
Design Firm, **Taylor & Ives, Inc.**
Art Director, **Alisa Zamir**
Designer, **Alisa Zamir**
Photographer, **William Taufic/Jon Ortner**
Copywriter, **Margot Witty**
Client, **Eastdil Realty, Inc.**
Eight colors on Reflections text, Curtis Gradations cover

2
Design Firm, **Knut Hartmann Design**
Art Director, **Roland Mehler**
Designer, **Roland Mehler**
Illustrator, **Roland Mehler**
Client, **Steigenberger Consulting**
Four process colors on Enhance Vanille 260g

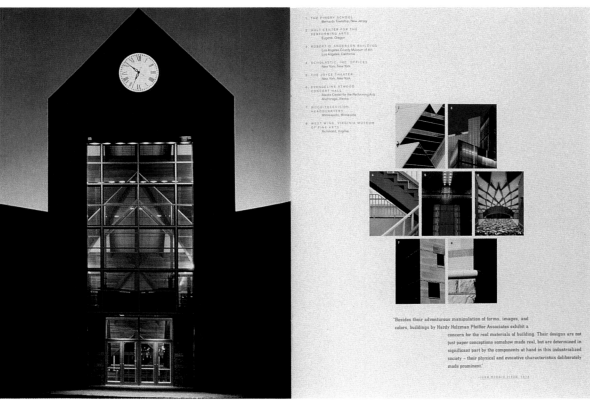

1
Design Firm, **Carbone Smolan Associates**
Art Director, **Ken Carbone**
Designer, **Allison Muench**
Copywriter, **Hardy, Holzman, Pfeiffer Associates**
Client, **Hardy, Holzman, Pfeiffer Associates**
Four process colors on Simpson Colorado
and Reflections

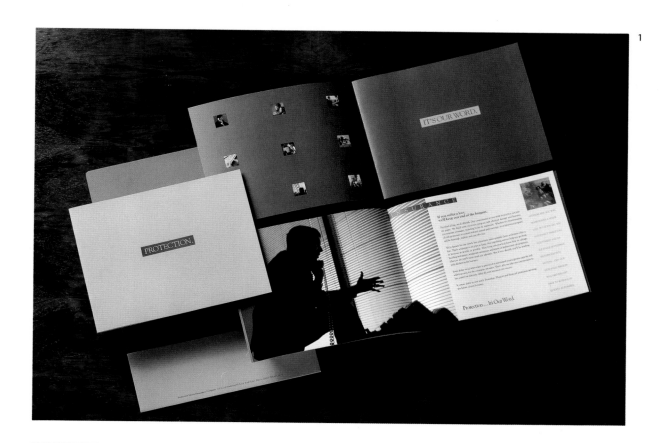

1
Design Firm, **Michael Stanard, Inc.**
Art Director, **Michael Stanard**
Designer, **Lisa Fingerhut**
Client, **Protection Mutual Insurance Co.**
Six colors

2
Design Firm, **Michael Stanard, Inc.**
Art Director, **Michael Stanard**
Designer, **Marcos Chavez**
Illustrator, **Marcos Chavez**
Client, **Sidney Eileen Miller**
Two colors

1

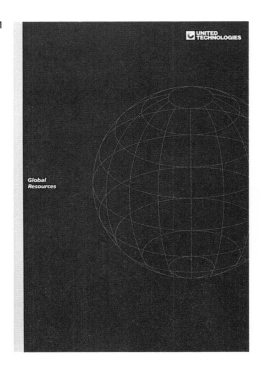

Global
Resources

Pratt & Whitney
Pratt & Whitney is the charter member of United Technologies Corporation. Founded in 1925 by Frederick B. Rentschler, Pratt & Whitney developed the Wasp engine after only eight months. Looking to the future, P&W immediately began designing the next generation engine.

Pioneering Powered Flight
Pratt & Whitney has been at the heart of powered flight since its founding. The company has pioneered and manufactured the most efficient engines of their time to power virtually every aircraft type. During the piston engine era, P&W supplied 173,618 Twin Wasp engines—more than any other aircraft engine in history–for fighters, bombers and commercial and military transports, including the DC-3.

After WWII, Pratt & Whitney's technology leadership enabled the company to surpass other manufacturers in the pursuit of gas turbine engines for propulsion. The first commercial Boeing 707 took flight in 1957, ushering in practical jet powered commercial aviation. It was powered by Pratt & Whitney engines. The military

version of that engine powered the first U.S. supersonic fighter and the B-52 bomber.

And, Pratt & Whitney engines power the world's fastest and highest flying airplane, the SR-71 "Blackbird," with an engine that was put into service an astounding 25 years ago.

Powering Aircraft Worldwide
Today, almost three quarters of the world's commercial jet transports are powered by Pratt & Whitney engines on over 1,000 airliners with some 370 airlines. In military aviation, Pratt & Whitney's Government Engine Business supplies power and support for U.S. and allied aircraft, including power plants for front-line fighters, the F-14, F-15 and F-16 and rocket motors for spacecraft, including the RL10, which has had a 100% reliability record for more than 25 years. Since 1948, Pratt & Whitney has produced more than 24,000 jet engines for the military.

The company has been developing and manufacturing engines in cooperation with companies in Europe and Asia-Pacific including International Aero Engines, a five-nation consortium created to develop a 25,000-pound thrust engine.

Pratt & Whitney Canada is the leading supplier of small gas turbine engines for business and commuter aircraft and helicopters, and Pratt & Whitney's Turbo Power and

Pratt & Whitney engines power nearly three-quarters of the world's commercial aircraft. The company has demonstrated its commitment to the industry as the only engine supplier with a new generation technology engine for all major thrust categories.

Pratt & Whitney-powered F-16 fighters have been purchased by the Air Forces of twelve nations; overall, Pratt & Whitney products are used by the military services of 68 nations.

16 17

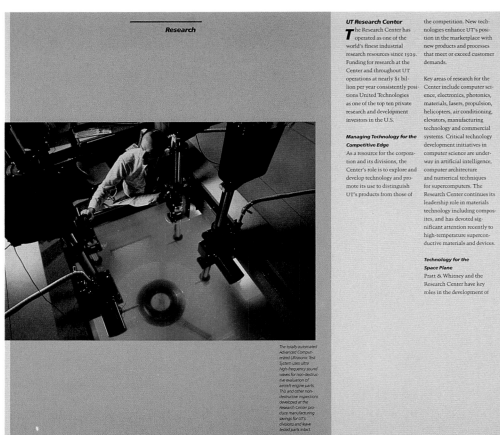

UT Research Center
The Research Center has operated as one of the world's finest industrial research resources since 1929. Funding for research at the Center and throughout UT operations at nearly $1 billion per year consistently positions United Technologies as one of the top ten private research and development investors in the U.S.

Managing Technology for the Competitive Edge
As a resource for the corporation and its divisions, the Center's role is to explore and develop technology and promote its use to distinguish UT's products from those of

the competition. New technologies enhance UT's position in the marketplace with new products and processes that meet or exceed customer demands.

Key areas of research for the Center include computer science, electronics, photonics, materials, lasers, propulsion, helicopters, air conditioning, elevators, manufacturing technology and commercial systems. Critical technology development initiatives in computer science are underway in artificial intelligence, computer architecture and numerical techniques for supercomputers. The Research Center continues its leadership role in materials technology including composites, and has devoted significant attention recently to high-temperature superconductive materials and devices.

Technology for the Space Plane
Pratt & Whitney and the Research Center have key roles in the development of

A remote temperature-measuring system pioneered at the United Technologies Research Center is a new diagnostic tool for product durability and efficiency improvement. A new system will incorporate lasers and glass fibers to measure temperatures in the Space Shuttle's main engines.

The totally automated Advanced Computerized Ultrasonic Test System uses ultra high-frequency sound waves for non-destructive evaluation of aircraft engine parts. This and other non-destructive inspections developed at the Research Center produce manufacturing savings for UT's divisions and leave tested parts intact.

4 5

1
Design Firm, **Richard Danne & Associates, Inc.**
Art Director, **Richard Danne**
Designer, **Gary Skeggs**
Copywriter, **H. Christian Conover**
Client, **United Technologies**
Seven colors on Warren Lustro gloss

This brochure is designed to be printed in ten different languages.

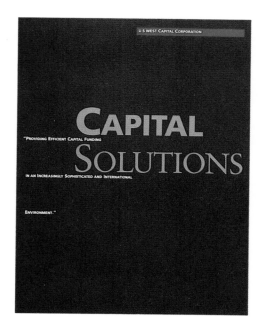

1
Design Firm, **Richard Danne & Associates, Inc.**
Art Director, **Richard Danne**
Designer, **Gary Skeggs**
Photographer, **Bill Farrell**
Copywriter, **John Stutz**
Client, **U.S. West Capital Corp.**
Five colors on Warren Lustro

1
Design Firm, **Akagi Design**
Art Director, **Doug Akagi**
Designer, **Doug Akagi/Kimberly Powell**
Photographer, **R.J. Muna**
Copywriter, **Shannon Kennedy/Lisa Suennen**
Client, **American Biodyne, Inc.**

2
Design Firm, **Platinum Design, Inc.**
Art Director, **Victoria Peslak**
Designer, **Kirsten Schumacher**
Photographer, **Bruce Plotkin**
Client, **Bruce Plotkin**
Four colors on Consort Royale Silk

1

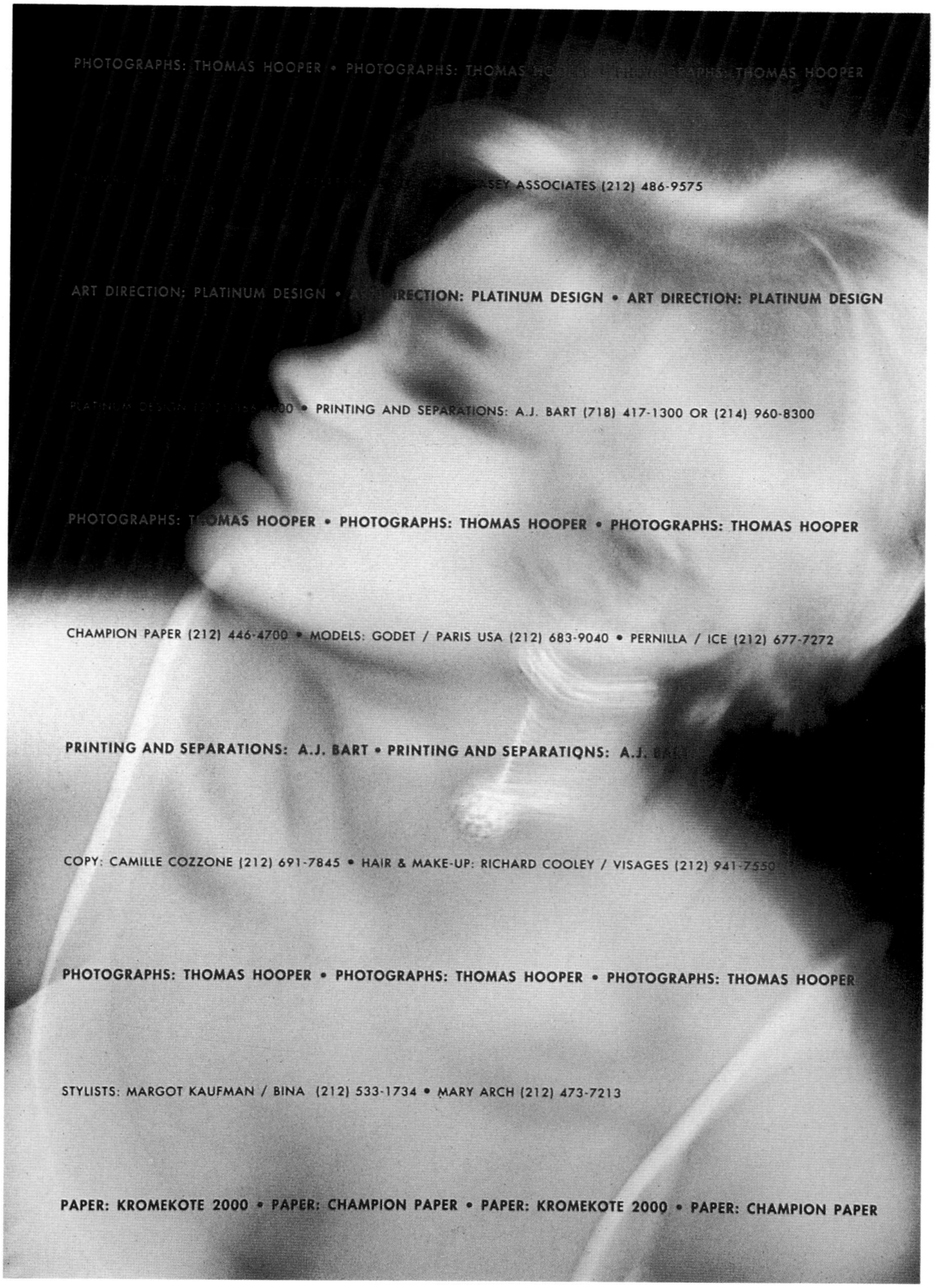
PHOTOGRAPHS: THOMAS HOOPER • PHOTOGRAPHS: THOMAS
THOMAS HOOPER
ASSOCIATES (212) 486-9575
ART DIRECTION: PLATINUM DESIGN •
RECTION: PLATINUM DESIGN • ART DIRECTION: PLATINUM DESIGN
PRINTING AND SEPARATIONS: A.J. BART (718) 417-1300 OR (214) 960-8300
PHOTOGRAPHS: THOMAS HOOPER • PHOTOGRAPHS: THOMAS HOOPER • PHOTOGRAPHS: THOMAS HOOPER
CHAMPION PAPER (212) 446-4700 • MODELS: GODET / PARIS USA (212) 683-9040 • PERNILLA / ICE (212) 677-7272
PRINTING AND SEPARATIONS: A.J. BART • PRINTING AND SEPARATIONS: A.J.
COPY: CAMILLE COZZONE (212) 691-7845 • HAIR & MAKE-UP: RICHARD COOLEY / VISAGES (212) 941-7550
PHOTOGRAPHS: THOMAS HOOPER • PHOTOGRAPHS: THOMAS HOOPER • PHOTOGRAPHS: THOMAS HOOPER
STYLISTS: MARGOT KAUFMAN / BINA (212) 533-1734 • MARY ARCH (212) 473-7213
PAPER: KROMEKOTE 2000 • PAPER: CHAMPION PAPER • PAPER: KROMEKOTE 2000 • PAPER: CHAMPION PAPER

1
Design Firm, **Platinum Design, Inc.**
Art Director, **Victoria Peslak**
Designer, **Wendi Horowitz**
Photographer, **Tom Hooper**
Copywriter, **Camille Cozzone**
Client, **Tom Hooper**
Five colors on Champion Kromekote 2000

1
Design Firm, **Frankfurt Gips Balkind**
Art Director, **Kent Hunter**
Designer, **Danielle Joffe**
Illustrator, **Frank Viva/Gene Greif/Dave Calver/**
Anthony Russo
Photographer, **Mark Jenkinson**
Copywriter, **Michael Clive**
Client, **Berlitz International, Inc.**
Six colors

Strategie: een kwestie van doen!

Hoe vindt u de geschikte manager?

Het succes van de organisatie staat of valt met de mensen. De geschikte manager vinden is moeilijk en tijdsintensief. De markt goed kennen is een vereiste. Toegang krijgen tot de doelgroep is essentieel. Ook dat is marketing.

De Adviesgroep Recrutering van VODW is gespecialiseerd in het werven en selecteren van directeuren, managers en vakspecialisten. Werkzaam op de gebieden van marketing-, commercieel- of financieel management. Deze doelgroep is vertrouwd met VODW. Dat werkt drempelverlagend en verhoogt de kwaliteit van de respons.

De specifieke aanpak van VODW vergroot de kans op resultaat. Op korte en lange termijn. Ook bij het vinden van geschikt management krijgt VODW zaken voor elkaar.

Recruteringsadviezen
Werving en selectie
Functie- en kandidaatprofielen
Organisatiestructuren
Functie- en taakomschrijvingen
Beloningssystemen
Selectie-instrumenten
Mediakeuze

Hoe krijgt u uw organisatie doelgericht in beweging?

Voor acceptatie van uw strategie door uw mensen is betrokkenheid van iedereen een voorwaarde. Alleen persoonlijke betrokkenheid kan leiden tot gedragsverandering. Daarbij zijn drie stappen wezenlijk. De strategie moet voor iedereen duidelijk zijn. Het management en de medewerkers moeten er zelf in geloven. En het management moet er zich als eerste naar gedragen.

VODW brengt organisaties in beweging. Marktgericht en in lijn met de gekozen strategie. Dat vereist een juiste afstemming van mensen, structuren en systemen. Oog hebben voor detail en op het juiste moment handelen. Het contact tussen markt en organisatie als meetpunt.

VODW is vertrouwd met het invoeren van marketing-processen in een onderneming. Dat verlangt eerst luisteren naar management en medewerkers. Daarna sturing en begeleiding door samenwerking. Zo komt ieder niveau van de organisatie in beweging. Doelgericht, conform de strategie.

Organisatie adviezen
Implementatie strategie
Marktgerichte organisatie-
ontwikkeling Interne communicatie
Kwaliteitsverbetering
Marketing-informatiesystemen
Marketingbegeleiding

1
Design Firm, **Samenwerkende Ontwerpers bv**
Design Consultancy
Art Director, **Andre Toet**
Designer, **Jan Paul de Vries**
Illustrator, **Josje van Koppen**
Photographer, **Freek van Arkel**
Client, **Verdonk, Otten, Dik & Wiecherinck**
Four colors

SELF-PROMOTIONAL

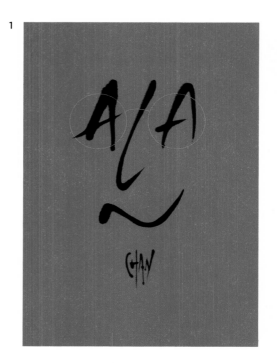

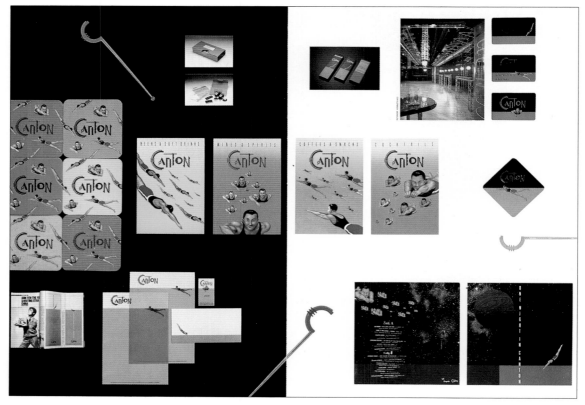

1
Design Firm, **Alan Chan Design Co.**
Art Director, **Alan Chan**
Designer, **Alan Chan/Phillip Leung/Peter Lo**
Photographer, **Sandy Lee/Johnny Koo**
Copywriter, **Hillery Binks**
Client, **Alan Chan Design Co.**
Five colors on art card, art paper

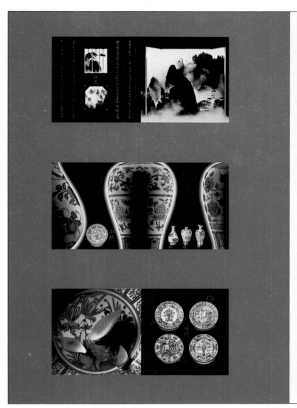

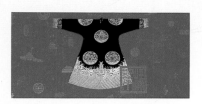

For the 1988 China Expo trade fair, exhibiting all sorts of goods from China and promoted by Seibu in Tokyo, a brochure was produced aimed at VIP groups, focusing on the exclusive and antique arts and crafts on show. • The distinctive cover featured the three Chinese characters denoting "China Expo", superimposed on a dragon's pearl, symbolising power and Chinese energy, a theme continued throughout the publication. Further, the red pearl surrounded by flames in the centre of a white cover signified Chinese energy in Japan. Gatefolds at front and back opened to reveal resplendent Mandarin robes — that of the Emperor in the front cover, that of the Empress at the back.

Thanks to his experience as co-owner of an antique shop, Eastern Origins, in the early 1980s, Chan was qualified to select from Seibu's collection those items which he thought would best project an authentic Chinese image for the fair. These included fine porcelain, clocks, lacquered furniture, carpets, Chinese paintings, artist's materials such as inkstone and brushes, Chinese tea and wine, and table linen. With habitual attention to detail, Chan spent 11 days in Tokyo with photographer Sandy Lee and two assistants, and art directed the photography personally. He positioned rain-splashed petals on porcelain, butterflies on carpets, and a tea set on a tablecloth, creating a mood as well as a scale for each shot and making it spiritually alive.

SEVENTY FIVE 七十五

The Optical Shop

In a first venture into product design in 1990, a series of spectacle cases was created for The Optical Shop, a leading optical chain with more than 40 branches in Hong Kong. Based on a Ching dynasty sharkskin case in Chan's private collection, the prototype succeeded in looking like a highly expensive accessory, but was actually made within the same production budget previously allocated to the former, quite ordinary cases. The idea was to create a spectacle case that people would be proud to display in public — on a conference table or in a restaurant. Also, for people with several pairs of spectacles, the cases were designed to stack one on top of the other for easy storage. Made in mock tortoiseshell, marble and plain colour, the case has a specially designed logotype in keeping with the nostalgic look of the packaging, and is signed by Alan Chan on the back.

ONE HUNDRED & THIRTEEN 一百零十三

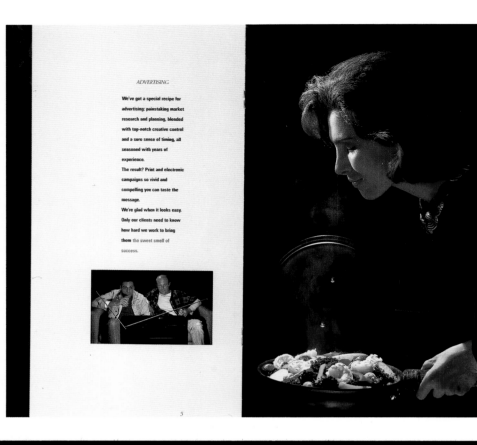

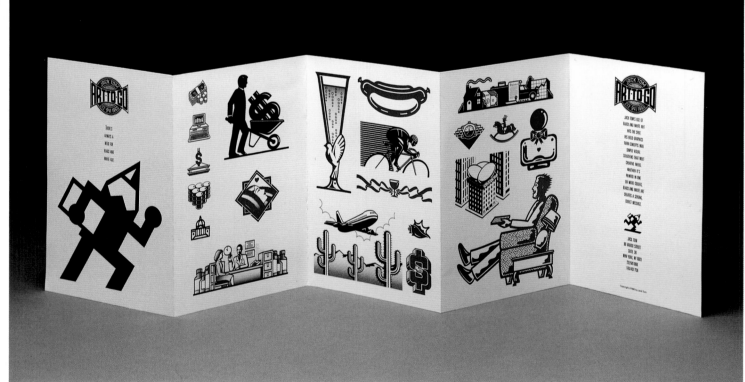

1
Design Firm, **Ascent Communications**
Art Director, **Allen Haeger**
Designer, **Allen Haeger**
Photographer, **Steve Gottlieb**
Client, **Ascent Communications**
Four process colors/six PMS colors

2
Design Firm, **Jack Tom Design**
Art Director, **Jack Tom**
Designer, **Jack Tom**
Illustrator, **Jack Tom**
Copywriter, **Jean Duperrault-Tom**
Client, **Jack Tom**
Three colors on Warren Lustro dull 100-lb. text

1
Design Firm, **Bernhardt Fudyma Design Group**
Art Director, **Craig Bernhardt/Janice Fudyma**
Designer, **Iris Brown**
Copywriter, **Barry Bohrer**
Client, **Bernhardt Fudyma Design Group**
Four process colors/two PMS colors and one dry pass of varnish on Strathmore
Grandee cover and Westvaco Inspirations text

This piece announces fifteen years in business. Everything in it relates in some way
to the number 15. Even the size of the brochure is 15 cm. by 15 cm.

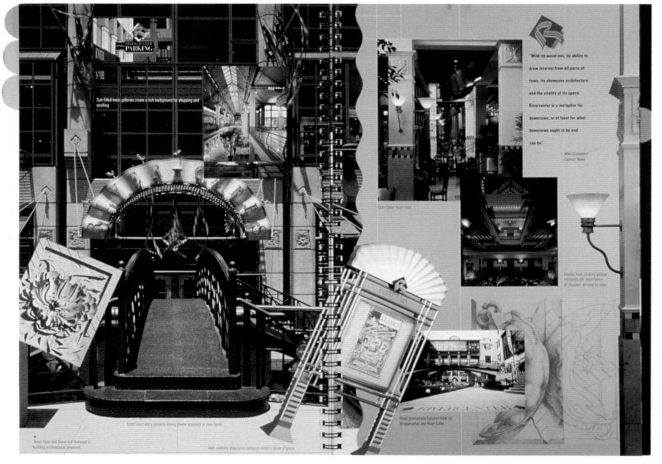

1
Design Firm, **Communication Arts, Inc.**
Art Director, **Richard Foy/Henry Beer**
Designer, **Mark Tweed**
Copywriter, **Richard Foy**
Client, **Communication Arts, Inc.**
Twelve colors on Quintessence

1
Design Firm, **Wilder-Fearn and Associates**
Art Director, **Gary Fearn**
Designer, **Wilder-Fearn and Associates**
Illustrator, **Wilder-Fearn and Associates**
Photographer, **Bray Ficken**
Copywriter, **Wilder-Fearn and Associates**
Client, **Wilder-Fearn and Associates**
Eight colors and varnish on Kromekote 2000

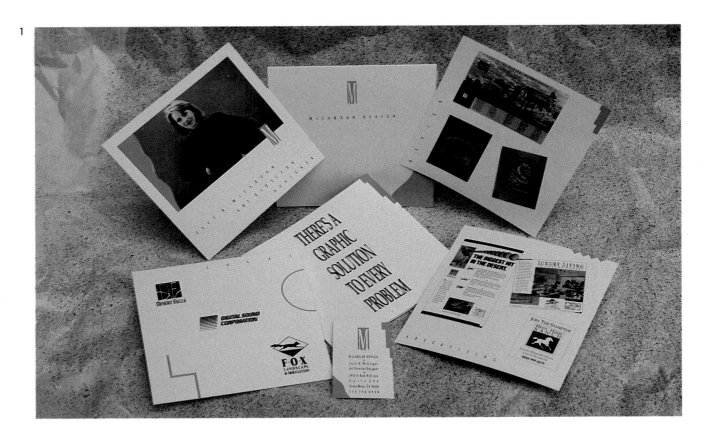

1
Design Firm, **McCargar Design**
Art Director, **Lucy McCargar**
Designer, **Lucy McCargar**
Copywriter, **Lucy McCargar**
Client, **McCargar Design**
Two colors on Lustro dull, die cut and folded

2
Design Firm, **McCargar Design**
Art Director, **Lucy McCargar**
Designer, **Lucy McCargar**
Photographer, **Elise Weinger**
Four process colors and a varnish on Centura gloss

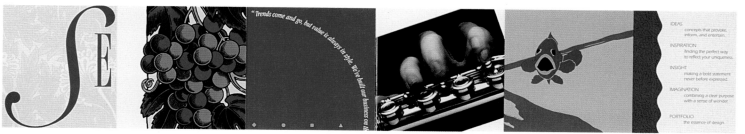

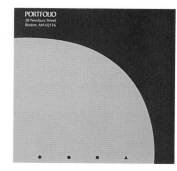

1
Design Firm, **Kollberg/Johnson Associates**
Art Director, **Penny Johnson/Gary Kollberg**
Designer, **Penny Johnson/Arthur Wang**
Photographer, **Jim Barber**
Copywriter, **Sharon Glaser**
Client, **Kollberg/Johnson Associates**
Three colors on 18-pt. Kromekote (folder), one
color on 12-pt. King James (pages)

2
Design Firm, **Portfolio**
Art Director, **Bonnie Mineo/Wendy Terry**
Designer, **Bonnie Mineo/Wendy Terry/
Busha Husak/Carmen Weltner**
Copywriter, **John Carroll/Neal Kane**
Client, **Portfolio**
Four process colors on 80-lb. Potlatch Karma gloss
cover

*Each panel is a section of a previous piece that
Portfolio had done for other clients.*

1

Soft 'n Gentle

Fort Howard Paper Company

Handi-Snacks

Kraft/General Foods

Premium Dip

Kraft/General Foods

Miller Special Premium Beer

Miller Brewing Company

1
Design Firm, **Design North, Inc.**
Art Director, **Richard Deardorff**
Designer, **Richard Deardorff**
Photographer, **James Wend**
Copywriter, **Don Kreger**
Client, **Design North, Inc.**
Nine colors on 100-lb. Lustre gloss cover

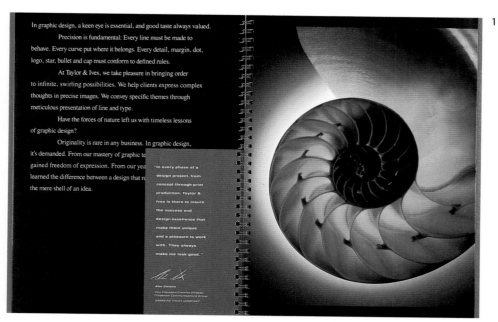

In graphic design, a keen eye is essential, and good taste always valued.

Precision is fundamental: Every line must be made to behave. Every curve put where it belongs. Every detail, margin, dot, logo, star, bullet and cap must conform to defined rules.

At Taylor & Ives, we take pleasure in bringing order to infinite, swirling possibilities. We help clients express complex thoughts in precise images. We convey specific themes through meticulous presentation of line and type.

Have the forces of nature left us with timeless lessons of graphic design?

Originality is rare in any business. In graphic design, it's demanded. From our mastery of graphic te[...] gained freedom of expression. From our yea[...] learned the difference between a design that r[...] the mere shell of an idea.

"In every phase of a design project, from concept through print production, Taylor & Ives is there to insure the success and design excellence that make them unique and a pleasure to work with. They always make me look good."

Alan Christie
Vice President/Creative Director
Corporate Communications Group
BANKERS TRUST COMPANY

Creative solutions come in many shapes and sizes. Ovals are ideal for packaging some messages. Circles have a role, too. At other times, it's hip to be square.

Experienced design consultants such as Taylor & Ives help you sort out the possibilities. We propose choices — governed by the ideas you want to express. We strive for economy, power, clarity and elegance. Diversity, within bounds. And impact.

Think about it:

It takes skill and experience to conceive and hatch a great annual report. When you succeed, the finished book is proudly presented for an entire year.

[...]ting documents have staying power. [...]relevance by summer or feel cold and out-of-[...]ok and feel right for all seasons.

[...]tain it, our clients never go away with egg

"You have done very handsome and creative work for us — from our corporate identity program to our annual reports. You are more than just a design firm — you are problem-solvers."

Peter Róna
President and Chief Executive Officer
IBJ SCHRODER BANK
& TRUST COMPANY

1
Design Firm, **Taylor & Ives, Inc.**
Art Director, **Alisa Zamir**
Designer, **Alisa Zamir**
Photographer, **Jim Barber**
Client, **Taylor & Ives, Inc.**
Six colors on Curtis Flannel cover, Reflections text

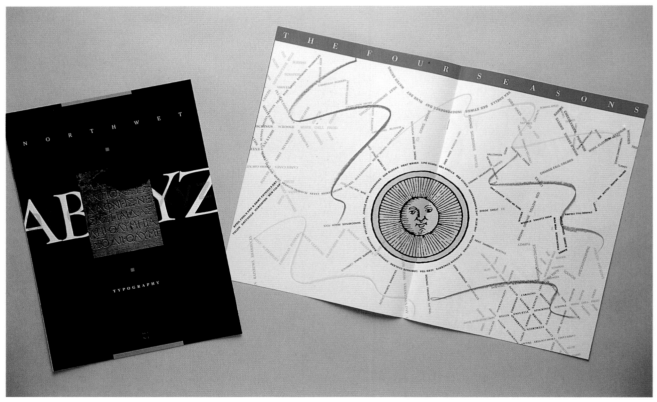

1
Design Firm, **Rick Eiber Design (RED)**
Art Director, **Rick Eiber**
Designer, **Rick Eiber and staff**
Photographer, **Rick Eiber (cover)**
Client, **Rick Eiber Design (RED)**
Four colors and four process color label (cover), three colors and tinted varnish
(inside), and five crayon colors added to center spread

1
Design Firm, **Rick Eiber Design (RED)**
Art Director, **Rick Eiber**
Designer, **Rick Eiber**
Photographer, **Ben Kerns/Doug Landreth**
Copywriter, **Rick Eiber/Sam Angeloff**
Client, **Rick Eiber Design (RED)**
Four colors, two varnishes, and silver on Chromolux and Ikonolux gloss cover
(inside cover), two colors, varnish, emboss and hotstamp (cover), four process
colors, gloss and dull varnishes (inside)

1
Design Firm, **Graphic Partners**
Art Director, **Ron Burnett**
Designer, **Ron Burnett**
Illustrator, **Douglas Watson**
Photographer, **Ian Atkinson**
Copywriter, **Elspeth Wills/Graham Duffy**
Client, **Graphic Partners**
Six colors on Consort Royal Silk

The unique style of these covers utilizes 3-D constructional illustrations. The cover of the brand brochure symbolizes origins of packaging and materials, while the corporate brochure cover represents definitive business life style.

2
Design Firm, **Emery/Poe Design**
Art Director, **David Poe**
Designer, **David Poe/Jonathan Mulcare**
Photographer, **Allan Krosnick**
Copywriter, **David Poe**
Client, **Emery/Poe Design**
Four process colors/three PMS colors on Simpson Cashmere and Simpson Evergreen cover

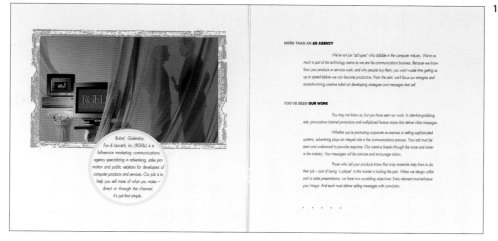

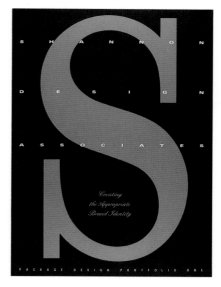

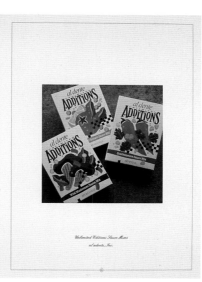

1
Design Firm, **RGF&L**
Art Director, **Candice Silva**
Designer, **Candice Silva**
Photographer, **Jim Green**
Client, **RGF&L**
Four process colors on Strathmore Pastelle cover

2
Design Firm, **Shannon Design Associates**
Art Director, **Amy Leppert**
Designer, **Amy Leppert**
Photographer, **D. Paul Rung**
Copywriter, **Michael Shannon**
Client, **Shannon Design Associates**
Four process colors/copper and varnish
on Reflections

MISCELLANEOUS

1
Design Firm, **Morla Design**
Art Director, **Jennifer Morla**
Designer, **Jennifer Morla**
Photographer, **Paul Franz-Moore**
Copywriter, **Leo Fermin**
Client, **San Francisco Airports Commission**
Printed on Kashmir Natural, Shasta gloss

1
Design Firm, **Morla Design**
Art Director, **Jennifer Morla**
Designer, **Jennifer Morla**
Illustrator, **Guy Billout**
Photographer, **Tom Tracy**
Copywriter, **Steven Falk**
Client, **San Francisco Airports Commission**
Four process colors on Mead Signature dull cover

*This piece focuses on business between East and
West, goods imported and exported and tourism.*

1

Al Mahmal Center

Shopping Center

Al Mahmal Center's seven-level complex comprises 21,000 square meters of Jeddah's most prestigious commercial space.

Each Level is arranged in gallery style around the atrium, with wide pedestrian walkways. This offers a comfortable and conducive environment for shoppers. It is further enhanced by the natural light filtering through the splendid glass ceiling, and the picturesque fountains and lush plants of the atrium.

A total leasable area of approximately 12,000 square meters is available in the shopping center. Set out in gallery format, it is highly adaptable and offers an ideal pattern for a variety of retail establishments.

Frameless flush glass runs the length of all interior store fronts, providing an unobstructed view of all window display areas.

The prime sites at ground level have an additional and unique feature of bullet-proof, tamper-free glass fronts on their exterior windows which eliminates the need for off-hours security grills. These sites also benefit from an elegant and shaded arcade which forms the perimeter of the building.

A series of 16 escalators set around the atrium transport shoppers from one level to another. Two elevators service shoppers at the West entrance, in addition to the two spectacular panoramic glass elevators overlooking the atrium at the North entrance of the building.

Entrances to the shopping center are provided on all four sides: on the East from King Abdul Aziz Street and, overhead, via a bridge linking the shopping center to the office tower; from the car park on the West via walkways at six different levels; from the plaza on the North side connecting the municipal parking lot with Al Mahmal, and from the South via the landscaped plaza leading shoppers to the grand main entrance at the front of the building.

1
Design Firm, **Alan Chan Design Co.**
Art Director, **Alan Chan**
Designer, **Alan Chan/Alvin Chan**
Photographer, **Sandy Lee/Stock photo**
Client, **Al Mahmal Center**
Four colors on art card, art paper

The die-cut on the cover of this brochure highlights the architecture of the shopping mall's main entrance.

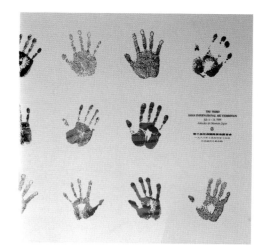

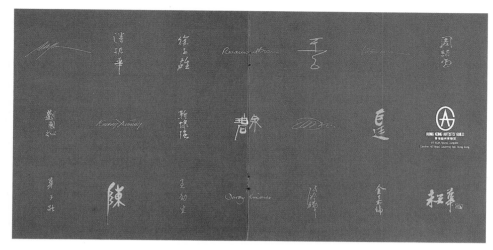

1
Design Firm, **Alan Chan Design Co.**
Art Director, **Alan Chan**
Designer, **Alan Chan**
Client, **Hong Kong Artists' Guild**
Five colors on matte art paper, art card

1
Design Firm, **Hornall Anderson Design Works**
Art Director, **John Hornall**
Designer, **John Hornall/Julia LaPine/**
Heidi Hatlestad/David Bates/Lian Ng
Copywriter, **Neil Starkman/Dennis Lone**
Client, **Roberts, Fitzmahan & Associates**
Four process colors on Evergreen matte/Lustro dull

*This set of four brochures is an effective educational
tool that teaches kids about the dangers of drugs
and alcohol.*

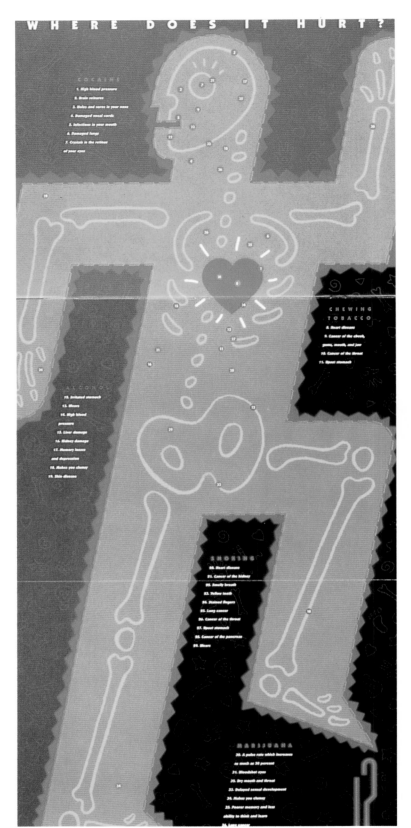

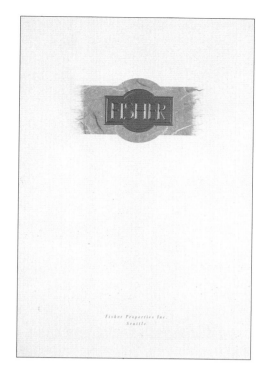

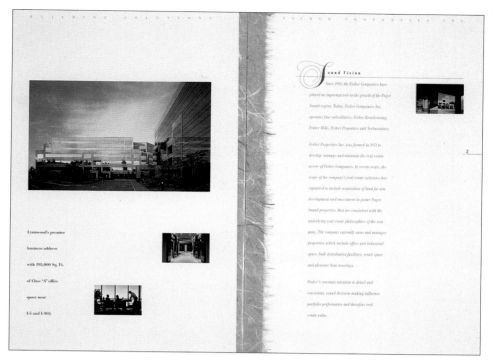

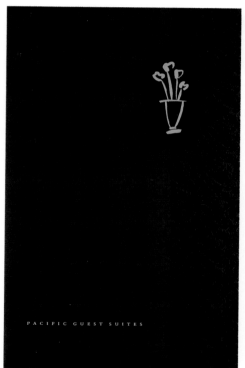

1
Design Firm, **Hornall Anderson Design Works**
Art Director, **Jack Anderson**
Designer, **Jack Anderson/Paula Cox**
Photographer, **James Frederick Housel**
Copywriter, **Jim Webb**
Client, **Fisher Properties**
Seven colors on Vintage/UV Ultra II

2
Design Firm, **Hornall Anderson Design Works**
Art Director, **Julia LaPine**
Designer, **Julia LaPine**
Photographer, **Raymond Gendreau**
Copywriter, **Brigid Healy Graham**
Client, **Pacific Guest Suites**
Three colors on Lustro dull Cream

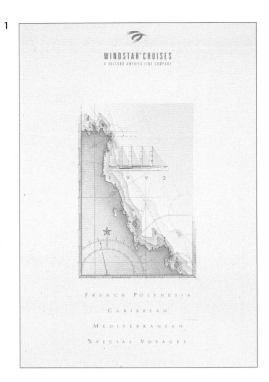

1
Design Firm, **Hornall Anderson Design Works**
Art Director, **Jack Anderson**
Designer, **Jack Anderson/Denise Weir**
Illustrator, **Bruce Morser**
Copywriter, **Joan Brown**
Client, **Windstar Cruises**
Six colors on Classic Laid cover, Avon White cover,
Sterling Web gloss text, Gilclear fly sheet

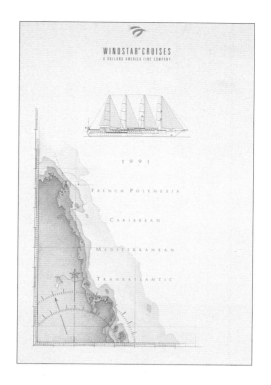

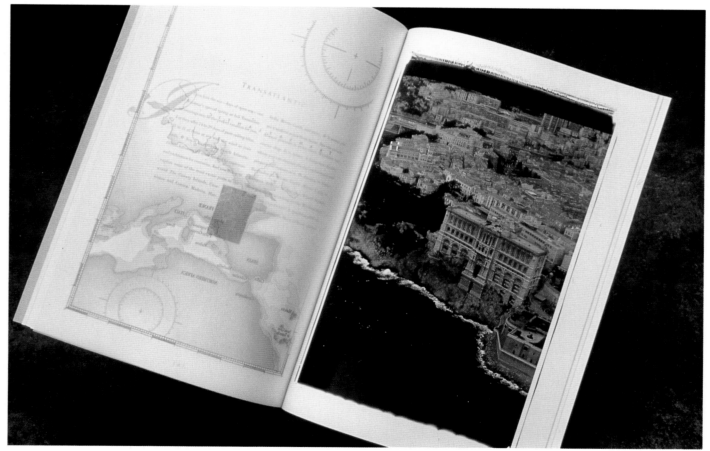

1
Design Firm, **Hornall Anderson Design Works**
Art Director, **Jack Anderson**
Designer, **Jack Anderson/Linda Muggli**
Illustrator, **Bruce Morser**
Copywriter, **Joan Brown/Pamela Mason-Davey**
Client, **Windstar Sail Cruises**
Six colors on Classic Laid cover, Avon Brilliant
cover, Sonoma gloss Book text, UV Ultra fly sheet

1
Design Firm, **Tyler Smith**
Art Director, **Tyler Smith**
Designer, **Tyler Smith**
Photographer, **Clint Clemens**
Copywriter, **Craig Walker**
Client, **Canyon View at Ventana**
Five colors on LOE Cream Warren

*This brochure was designed before any construction
had taken place. The environmental concept is
expressed by "Ansel Adams"-type photography.*

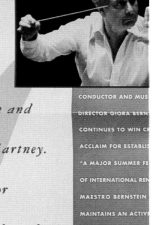

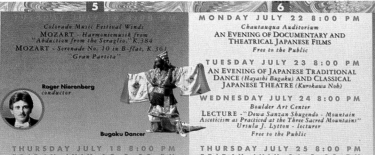

1
Design Firm, **Communication Arts, Inc.**
Art Director, **Henry Beer**
Designer, **Hugh Enockson**
Client, **Colorado Music Festival**
Six colors on Centura gloss

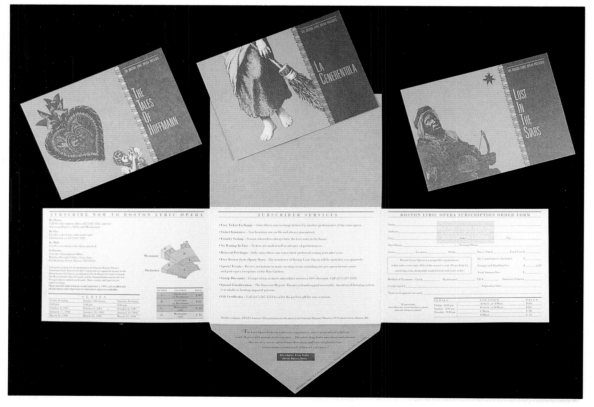

1
Design Firm, **Hill, Holliday Design**
Art Director, **Michael Perfetto**
Designer, **Jessica Godbey**
Photographer, **Peter Vanderwarker**
Copywriter, **Boston Lyric Opera**
Client, **Boston Lyric Opera**
Four colors on Zellerbach Wausau Royal
Fiber white

1
Design Firm, **Pat Gorman/Manhattan Design**
Art Director, **Pat Gorman/Frank Olinsky**
Designer, **Pat Gorman/Frank Olinsky**
Illustrator, **Native pattern by Chief Raoni**
Photographer, **Sue Cunningham**
Client, **The Rainforest Foundation**
Five colors on Recycled 10-pt uncoated

1
Design Firm, **Donovan and Green**
Art Director, **Michael Donovan**
Designer, **Michael Donovan/Jenny Barry/**
Barbara Tanis/Clint Morgan
Illustrator, **Carlos Diniz**
Photographer, **Peter Aaron/Neil Selkirk**
Copywriter, **David Borstin/Jim Kiewel**
Client, **Olympia & York Retail Development Co.**
Five colors and two varnishes on 100-lb.
Ikonorex dull

2
Design Firm, **Communication Arts, Inc.**
Art Director, **Henry Beer**
Designer, **David A. Shelton**
Client, **Western Development Corp.**
Three colors on Speckletone Cordtone Natural
cover

Registered emboss on cover with clear foil.

2
Design Firm, **Communication Arts, Inc.**
Art Director, **Henry Beer**
Designer, **David A. Shelton**
Illustrator, **Karmen Effenberger Thompson**
Photographer, **Richard Peterson**
Copywriter, **Ginny Hoyle**
Client, **Rouse-Arizona Center, Inc.**
Six colors on Quintessence

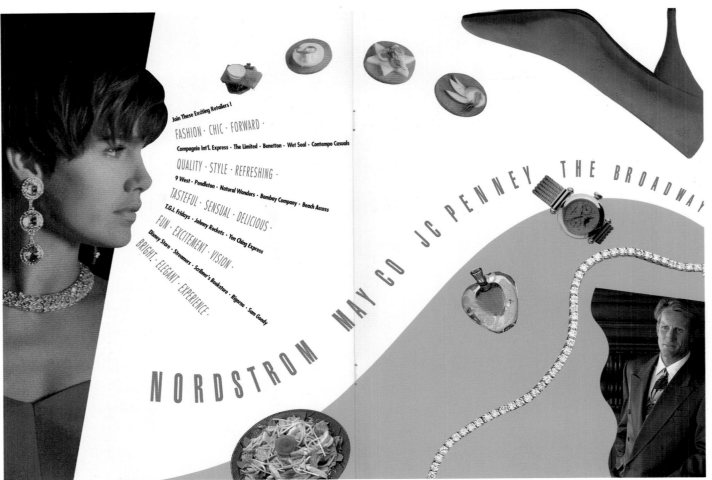

1
Design Firm, **Communcation Arts, Inc.**
Art Director, **Richard Foy**
Designer, **T. Keith Harley**
Photographer, **Donahue Schriber**
Copywriter, **Communication Arts, Inc.**
Client, **Donahue Schriber**
Four colors on Quintessence gloss 100-lb. cover

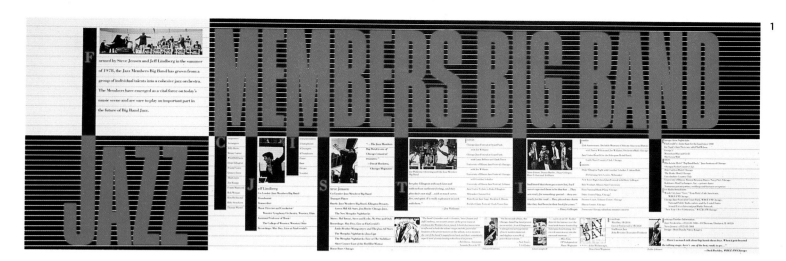

1
Design Firm, **Porter/Matjasich & Associates**
Art Director, **Bette Randa**
Designer, **Bette Randa**
Photographer, **Jazz Members Big Band**
Client, **Jazz Members Big Band**
Two colors and a spot varnish

2
Design Firm, **Sayles Graphic Design**
Art Director, **John Sayles**
Designer, **John Sayles**
Copywriter, **Wendy Lyons**
Client, **Iowa Medical Society**
Two colors on James River Reetreve

This fund-raising piece for a political action committee of doctors was mailed in a triangular box. Inside, a brochure and vial of Sweetarts candy help to drive home the headline "The Wrong Legislation could be a Bitter Pill to Swallow."

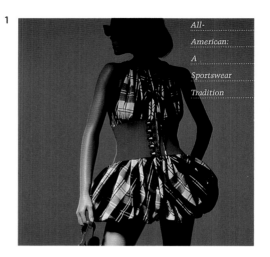

1
Design Firm, **Richard Danne & Associates, Inc.**
Art Director, **Richard Danne**
Designer, **Richard Danne/Kurt Jennings**
Photographer, **Taishi Hirokawa**
Copywriter, **Laura Sinderbrand**
Client, **Fashion Institute of Technology**
Printed on Northwest Vintage

A highly acclaimed chef prepares delectable six course dinners for the pleasure of Timberhill guests, using locally-grown produce, fish, and fowl in the ever-changing menu. Timberhill's own herb gardens supply many of the ingredients; and breads, pastries and desserts are created on the premises.

FINE

The open and airy dining room frames the best of the great outdoors — the lush hills, spectacular sunsets, the towering redwoods. To set the mood for romance, candlelit tables for two are graced with fine china, fine crystal, and sterling silver.

CUISINE

A selection from the generous stock of Northern California's fine wines compliments this epicurean experience, and a glass of port fireside in the lodge tops off a memorable evening.

1
Design Firm, **Colonna, Farrell: Design Associates**
Art Director, **Tony Auston**
Designer, **Chris Baldwin**
Illustrator, **Michele Manning**
Photographer, **Monica Lee**
Client, **Timberhill Ranch**
Four colors on Evergreen

2
Design Firm, **Donovan and Green**
Art Director, **Nancye Green/Julie Riefler**
Designer, **Julie Riefler**
Illustrator, **Greg Dearth/The Drake Manuscript**
Copywriter, **Gaye Torrance**
Client, **The Carvill Group**
Four colors and two varnishes on Three Crowns, Ikonolux, and Zanders Elephant Hide

A Matter of Ethics:

Truth runs
          for daylight.
Keeping it in the dark
is difficult,
if not
          impossible.

Tell
    the truth,
        even when it hurts!

"You taught me to run my
operation so we have
nothing to hide, not as if we
have nothing to hide."

1
Design Firm, **The Weller Institute for the Cure
of Design, Inc.**
Art Director, **Don Weller**
Designer, **Don Weller**
Illustrator, **Don Weller**
Copywriter, **Ron Gossling**
Client, **Communication Counsel of America**
Four process colors on Karma Natural

2
Design Firm, **Marsha Drebelbis Studio**
Art Director, **Marsha Drebelbis**
Designer, **Marsha Drebelbis**
Illustrator, **Marsha Drebelbis**
Client, **The Greenhouse**
Two PMS colors and foil stamping

*This holiday brochure features an embossed
illustration that is reminiscent of the white latticework
architecture at this elegant facility.*

1
Design Firm, **Art Chantry Design**
Art Director, **Art Chantry**
Designer, **Art Chantry**
Illustrator, **Carl Smool**
Client, **Pacific Northwest Art Exposition**
Four colors on newsprint

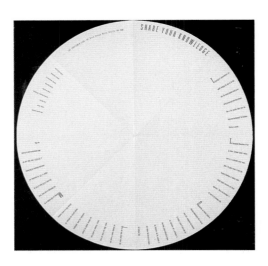

1
Design Firm, **Art Chantry Design**
Art Director, **Scott Herren**
Designer, **Art Chantry**
Copywriter, **John Koval**
Client, **Northwest Guild of Printing
House Craftsmen**
Four PMS colors (dayglo and black)

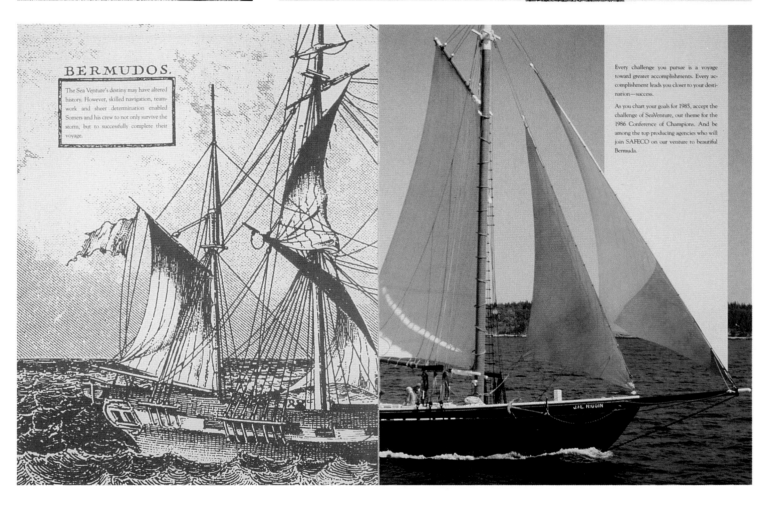

BERMUDOS.

The Sea Venture's destiny may have altered history. However, skilled navigation, teamwork and sheer determination enabled Somers and his crew to not only survive the storm, but to successfully complete their voyage.

Every challenge you pursue is a voyage toward greater accomplishments. Every accomplishment leads you closer to your destination—success.

As you chart your goals for 1985, accept the challenge of SeaVenture, our theme for the 1986 Conference of Champions. And be among the top producing agencies who will join SAFECO on our venture to beautiful Bermuda.

1
Design Firm, **Art Chantry Design**
Art Director, **Art Chantry**
Designer, **Art Chantry**
Photographer, **Tom Collicott**
Copywriter, **Susan Knox**
Client, **Safeco Insurance Companies**
Six colors

This piece is a launch for an annual in-house campaign to increase sales through a free-vacation package as an incentive.

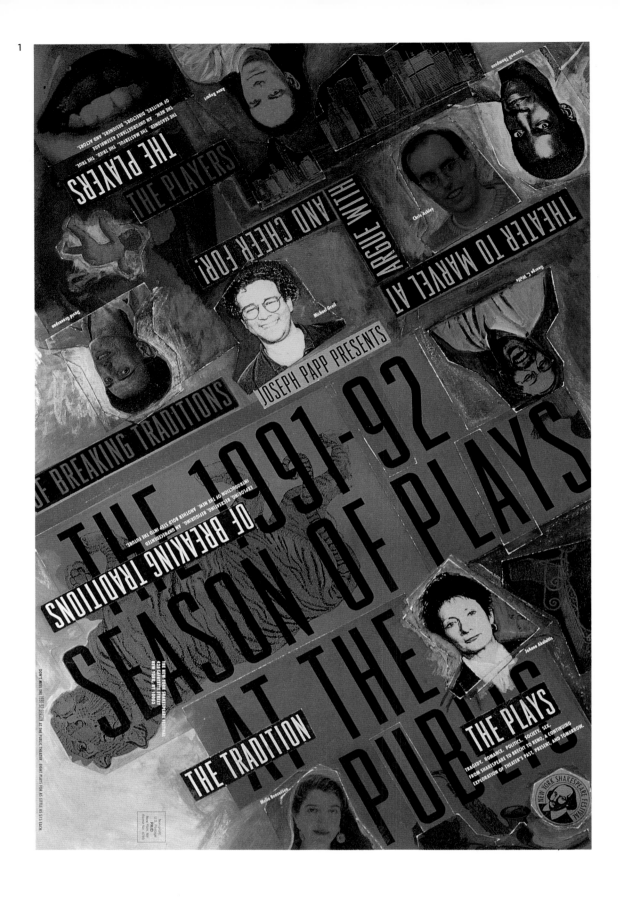

1
Design Firm, **Paul Davis Studio**
Art Director, **Paul Davis**
Designer, **Paul Davis/Lisa Mazur**
Illustrator, **Paul Davis**
Photographer, **Paul Davis/Martha Swope**
Copywriter, **Ann Murphy**
Client, **New York Shakespeare Festival**
Four process colors

1
Design Firm, **Paul Davis Studio**
Art Director, **Paul Davis**
Designer, **Mariana Ochs/Paul Davis**
Illustrator, **Paul Davis**
Photographer, **George E. Joseph/Martha Swope/**
Carol Rosegg
Copywriter, **Ann Murphy**
Client, **New York Shakespeare Festival**
Four process colors on Gilbert Esse Recycled

1
Design Firm, **DMCD**
Art Director, **Tom Neilson**
Designer, **Tom Neilson**
Copywriter, **Donna Franklin**
Client, **Du Pont Imaging**
Five colors on Reflections

2
Design Firm, **Pinkhaus Design Corp.**
Art Director, **Joel Fuller**
Designer, **Laura Latham**
Photographer, **South Florida ASMP**
Copywriter, **Frank Cunningham**
Client, **South Florida Chapter ASMP**
Four process colors on Signature gloss

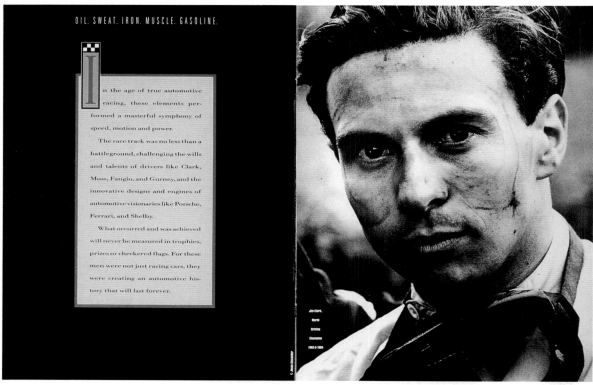

1
Design Firm, **Muller & Co.**
Art Director, **John Muller**
Designer, **John Muller/Scott Chapman**
Photographer, **Mike Regnier**
Copywriter, **John Krueger**
Client, **Sport Vintage Racing Association**
Four colors on 60-lb. gloss cover Signature
from Mead

Bristol-Myers Squibb Pharmaceutical Group
Summer 1991
TeamOne
In this issue:
The Dynamic Marketplace of Eastern Europe
Captopril Finishing Suite in the USSR
Executive Interview: Barry W. Wilson
Profile of the Eastern European Bloc Pharmaceutical Customer
Fosinopril: The New ACE Inhibitor
C O M P E T I N G T O G E T H E R

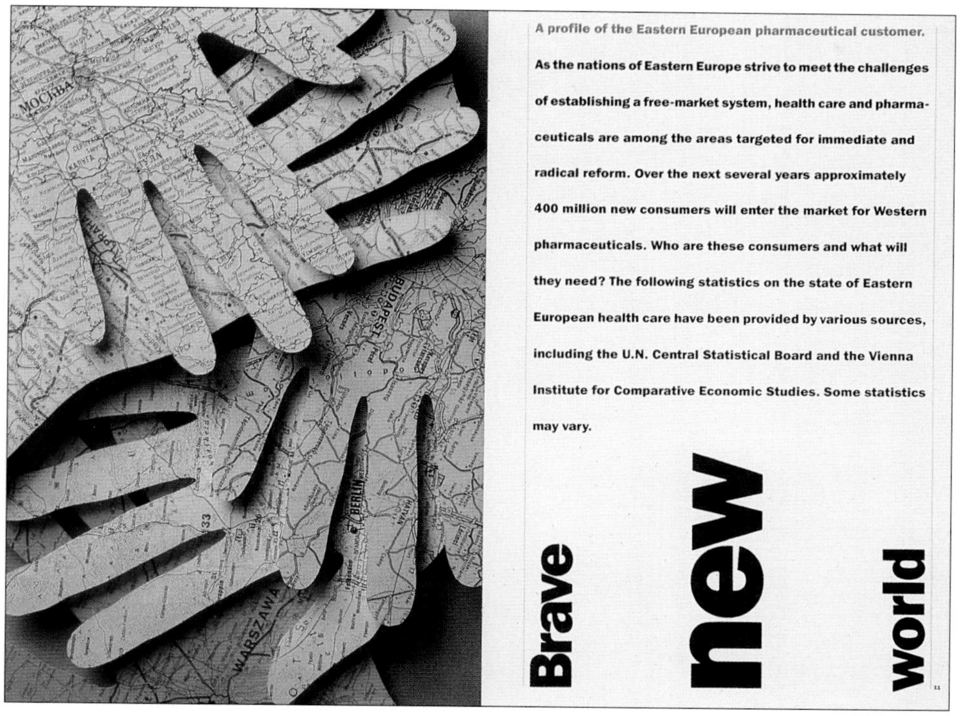
A profile of the Eastern European pharmaceutical customer.
As the nations of Eastern Europe strive to meet the challenges of establishing a free-market system, health care and pharmaceuticals are among the areas targeted for immediate and radical reform. Over the next several years approximately 400 million new consumers will enter the market for Western pharmaceuticals. Who are these consumers and what will they need? The following statistics on the state of Eastern European health care have been provided by various sources, including the U.N. Central Statistical Board and the Vienna Institute for Comparative Economic Studies. Some statistics may vary.
Brave
new
world

1

LODGE

2

1
Design Firm, **Clarion Marketing and Communications**
Art Director, **Robert Frankle**
Designer, **Robert Frankle**
Photographer, **Charlotte Raymond**
Four colors on Ikonofix

2
Design Firm, **Communication Arts, Inc.**
Art Director, **Richard Foy**
Designer, **T. Keith Harley**
Illustrator, **Stan Doctor**
Photographer, **Nicholas DeSciose/David Muench**
Copywriter, **Richard Foy/Jonathon Levi**
Client, **Kensington Land Investment Partners**
Six colors on Quintessence

1

Design Firm, **Walter McCord Graphic Design**
Art Director, **Walter McCord/Albert Leggett**
Designer, **Walter McCord/Albert Leggett**
Photographer, **Albert Leggett**
Copywriter, **Albert Leggett**
Client, **Albert Leggett Photography**
Four process colors

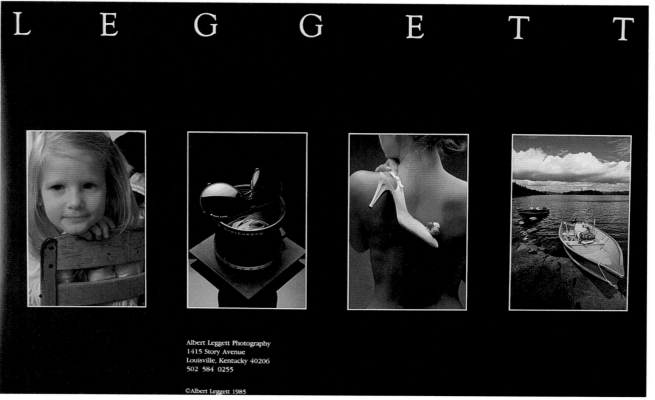

1
Design Firm, **Walter McCord Graphic Design**
Art Director, **Walter McCord/Albert Leggett**
Designer, **Walter McCord/Albert Leggett**
Photographer, **Albert Leggett**
Copywriter, **Albert Leggett**
Client, **Albert Leggett Photography**
Four process colors

2
Design Firm, **Walter McCord Graphic Design**
Art Director, **Albert Leggett**
Designer, **Albert Leggett**
Type Director, **Walter McCord**
Photographer, **Albert Leggett**
Copywriter, **Albert Leggett**
Client, **Albert Leggett Photography**

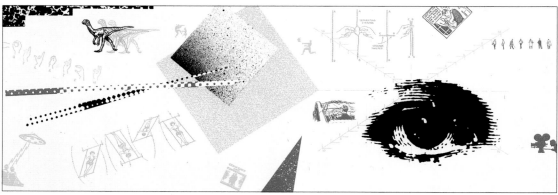

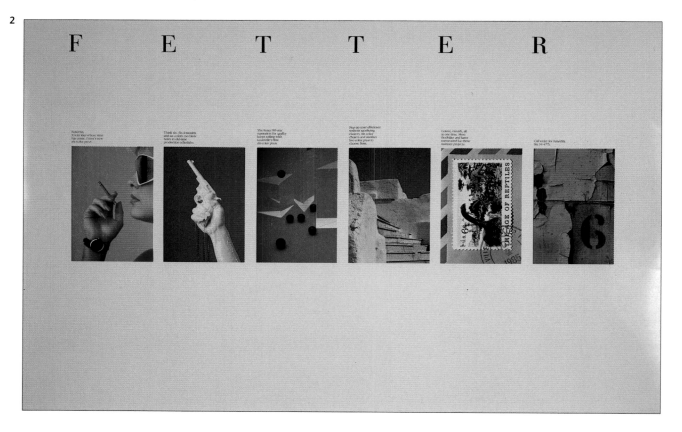

1
Design Firm, **Walter McCord Graphic Design**
Art Director, **Walter McCord**
Designer, **Walter McCord**
Illustrator, **Walter McCord**
Copywriter, **Karen Fox**
Client, **Nationwide Papers**
Four colors on Potlatch Karma

2
Design Firm, **Walter McCord Graphic Design**
Art Director, **Walter McCord**
Designer, **Walter McCord**
Photographer, **Walter McCord**
Copywriter, **Bob Gaeta**
Client, **Fetter Printing**
Four process colors on Champion Kromekote

Looking through
my bedroom window,
out into the moonlight and the
unending smoke-colored snow,
I could see the lights in the windows
of all the other houses
on our hill and hear
the music rising from them up the
long, steadily falling night.

Dylan Thomas
A Child's Christmas in Wales

Merry Christmas from
Fetter Printing Company

1
Design Firm, **Walter McCord Graphic Design**
Art Director, **Walter McCord**
Designer, **Walter McCord**
Photographer, **Walter McCord**
Copywriter, **Dylan Thomas**
Client, **Fetter Printing**
Four process colors on Mead Lustro Offset
Enamel dull

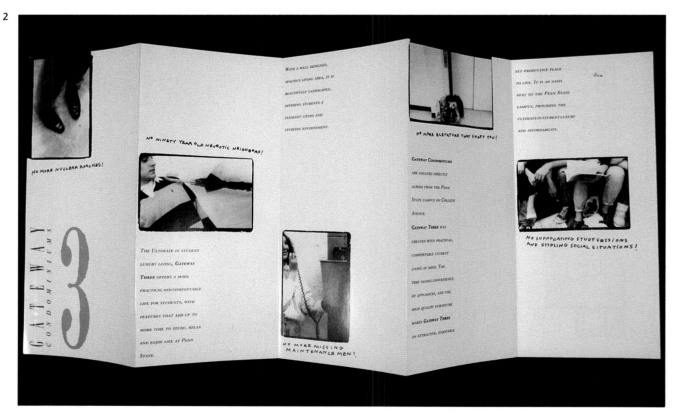

1
Design Firm, **Sommese Design**
Art Director, **Lanny Sommese/Kristin Breslin**
Designer, **Kristin Breslin**
Photographer, **Lanny Sommese**
Client, **HFL Corp.**
Four process colors with a one-color insert

*The cover motif on the folder is taken from
architectural details of the building. A circular die-cut
is punched through the cover to expose a photo of
the architect's model of the building.*

2
Design Firm, **Sommese Design**
Art Director, **Kristin Breslin**
Designer, **Kristin Breslin**
Photographer, **Kristin Breslin**
Copywriter, **Kristin Breslin**
Client, **HFL Corp.**
Three colors

"The Crowd" is the culminating work of a long series of street scenes. But here the passers-by assume a new role as members of humanity and the union of people is in itself the theme.

The movement of a crowd is one of unparalleled continuous metamorphosis — a prerequisite for sculpture I believe. Fascinating like a procession of clouds or ocean waves the diabolical dance of flames, the crowd, by its human significance, transcends all these to attain drama.

A link with my sculptured landscapes and their clefts and crevices seems possible but the oceanic world is also present. A sea of people. However I am first and foremost a city-dweller and the constant throng of my fellow-beings is my daily bread.

Raymond Mason

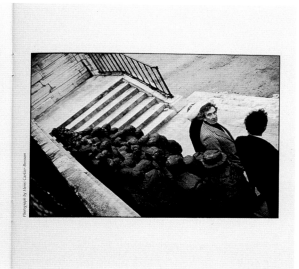

Photograph by Henri Cartier-Bresson

Raymond Mason has great thumbs for sculpture, smashed flat and bent double back from countless days of plying, gouging and smoothing material into form. Mason's primary material is plaster, and in his hands it can become anything. He mixes it in half of a rubber ball, obtained from a toy vendor in the park near his Paris studio. The studio is a white world filled with monumental work in progress. Soft light from the overhead skylight fills the space. Plaster dust like freshly fallen snow covers the floor. Anyone leaving the studio must carefully wipe his feet. For Mason, plaster is the solution for every problem, from mending the skylight to binding his armatures together. In his hands, plaster magically becomes delicate lettuce leaves or bruised fruit, punched in faces of an anonymous crowd or branches of a near life-size tree. — Sometimes when he has chosen to abandon bronze and the job of modeling is complete, Raymond puts away his plaster and rubber mixing ball and wheels in a cart loaded with many jars of multi-colored vinyl paint. My fantasy is that he arms himself with brushes, goes to the electrical board of his studio/laboratory and pulls down on the handle of a giant circuit switch à la Dr. Frankenstein. It sends a super-charged volt of pure color onto the first plaster shapes. — Raymond the artist/inventor is driven with excitement, adding more color everywhere. to noses, hats, elbows, crotches, cobblestones, chimneys, window pots, fists, armpits, clouds. At this point Raymond, who in addition to his sculptor's hands and painter's eye possesses a

1
Design Firm, **Patterson Wood Partners**
Art Director, **Tom Wood**
Designer, **Tom Wood**
Photographer, **Gloria Baker**
Copywriter, **Mary Anne Costello**
Three colors and metallic on Warren LOE

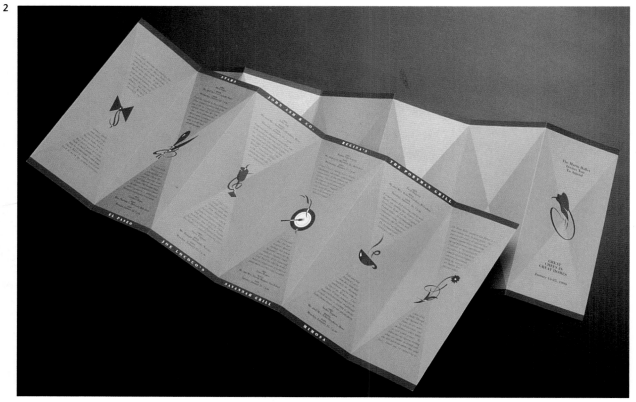

1
Design Firm, Colonna, Farrell: Design Associates
Art Director, **Tony Auston**
Designer, **Tony Auston**
Illustrator, **Mike Gray**
Client, **Napa Valley Vintners Association**
Two PMS colors on Speckletone

2
Design Firm, **Sackett Design**
Art Director, **Mark Sackett**
Designer, **Mark Sackett**
Illustrator, **Mike Takagi**
Client, **Marin Ballet**
Three colors on 100-lb. Quintessence dull

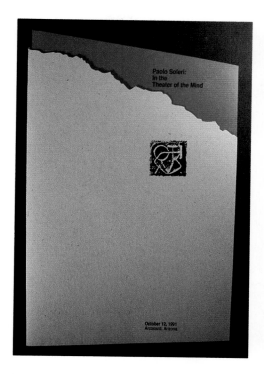

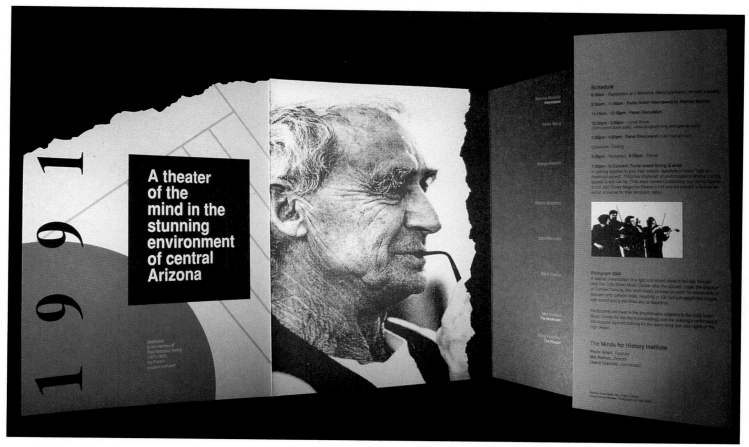

1
Design Firm, **Rowley Associates, Inc.**
Art Director, **James R. Rowley**
Designer, **Lanie Gotcher**
Photographer, **Robert Vance Blosser**
Copywriter, **Debra Giannini**
Client, **Cosanti Foundation**
Two colors on 80-lb. Speckletone

This piece features custom die-cutting and opaque
white ink added to increase opacity.

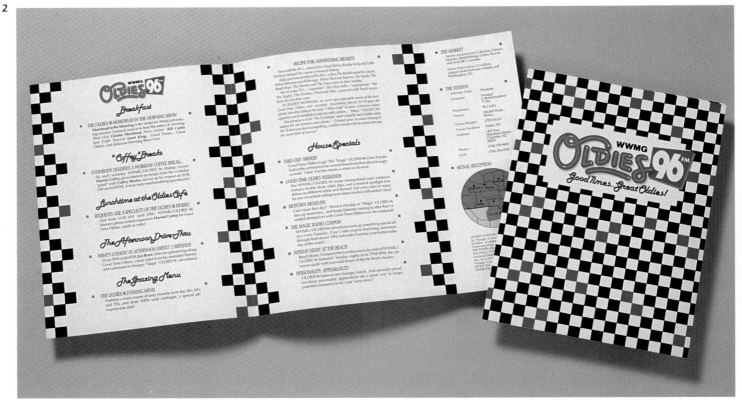

1
Design Firm, **Sabin Design**
Art Director, **Marilee Barkert**
Designer, **Tracy Sabin**
Illustrator, **Tracy Sabin**
Copywriter, **Marilee Barkert**
Client, **Fashion Valley**
Four process colors on Quintessence

This brochure features windows that open.

2
Design Firm, **Steve Galit Associates**
Art Director, **Christine Pearson**
Designer, **Christine Pearson**
Client, **Voyager Communications**
Three PMS colors on Kromekote

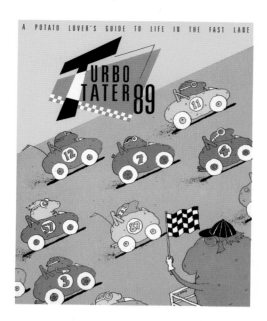

Design Firm, **Lee Reedy Design Associates, Inc.**
Art Director, **Lee Reedy**
Designer, **Lee Reedy**
Illustrator, **Lee Reedy**
Copywriter, **Nancy McCarthy**
Client, **The Potato Board**
Three colors on LOE dull

Design Firm, **Frankfurt Gips Balkind**
Creative Director, **Evan Moon**
Designer, **Steven Fabrizio**
Copywriter, Cindy Ris
Client, **Battery Park City Authority**
Six colors

1
Design Firm, **Platinum Design, Inc.**
Art Director, **Vickie Peslak/Melissa Norton**
Designer, **Vickie Peslak/Melissa Norton**
Illustrator, **Sergio Baradat**
Client, **U.S. News and World Report**

2
Design Firm, **Platinum Design, Inc.**
Art Director, **Victoria Peslak**
Designer, **Kirsten Schumacher**
Client, **Harper's Bazaar**
Four colors on Quintessence

1
Design Firm, **Platinum Design, Inc.**
Art Director, **Victoria Peslak**
Designer, **Kirsten Schumacher**
Illustrator, **Sergio Baradat**
Client, **Business Week Magazine**
Four colors on Quintessence

2
Design Firm, **Platinum Design, Inc.**
Art Director, **Victoria Peslak**
Designer, **Sandy Quinn**
Illustrator, **Robert Burger**
Client, **Business Week Magazine**
Four colors on Kromekote

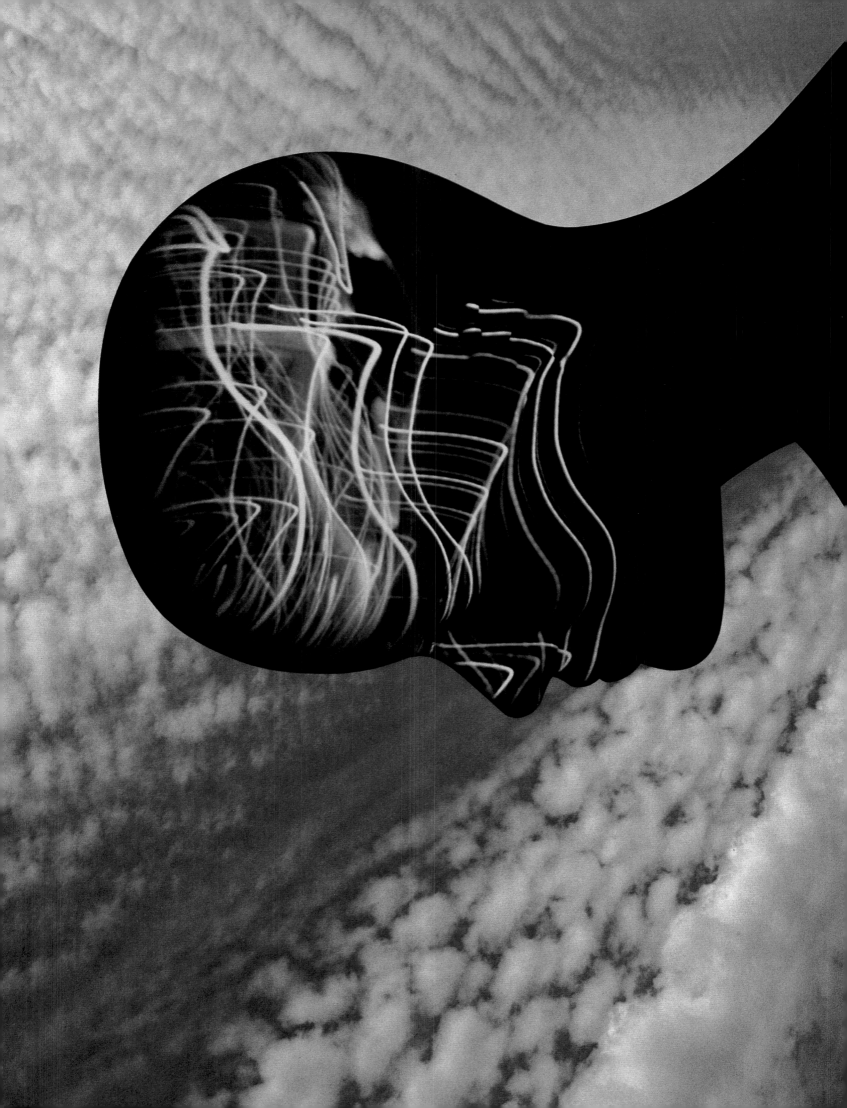

COVERS

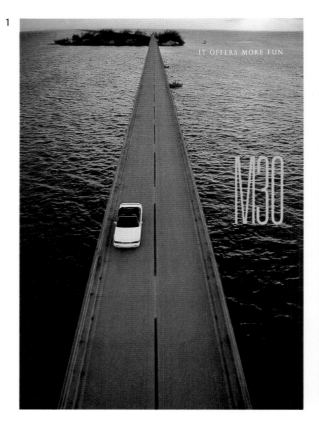

1
Design Firm, **Hill Holliday Design**
Art Director, **Vic Cevoli**
Designer, **John Avery**
Photographer, **Clint Clemens**
Copywriter, **Neill Ray**
Client, **Nissan Infiniti 1992 M30 Model**
Four colors on Vintage

2
Design Firm, **Hill Holliday Design**
Art Director, **Vic Cevoli**
Designer, **John Avery**
Photographer, **Clint Clemens**
Copywriter, **Neill Ray**
Client, **Nissan Infiniti 1992 Q45 Model**
Four colors on Vintage

3
Design Firm, **Hill Holliday Design**
Art Director, **Vic Cevoli**
Designer, **John Avery**
Photographer, **Clint Clemens**
Copywriter, **Neill Ray**
Client, **Nissan Infiniti 1992 G20 Model**
Four colors on Vintage

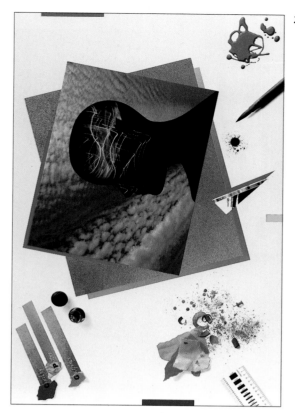

1
Design Firm, **Images**
Art Director, **Walter McCord/Julius Friedman**
Designer, **Walter McCord/Julius Friedman**
Client, **Cordage Paper**
Duotone and tritone demo on Potlatch Karma

2
Design Firm, **Walter McCord Graphic Design**
Art Director, **Walter McCord/Julius Friedman**
Designer, **Walter McCord/Julius Friedman**
Illustrator, **Walter McCord**
Photographer, **Joe Boone**
Client, **Cordage Papers**

3
Design Firm, **Walter McCord Graphic Design**
Art Director, **Walter McCord/Julia Comer**
Designer, **Walter McCord/Julia Comer**
Photographer, **Chuck Carlton**
Client, **Jasper Oriental Rugs**
Four process colors on Champion Kromekote

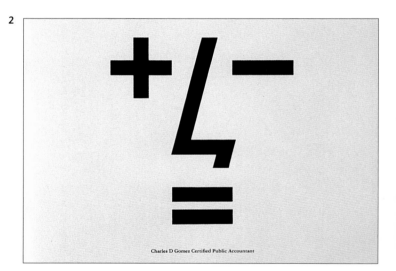

1
Design Firm, **Art Chantry Design**
Art Director, **Art Chantry**
Designer, **Art Chantry**
Photographer, **Jim Ball/Kevin Westenberg**
Copywriter, **Beth Brooks**
Client, **The Empty Space Theatre**
One color on coated paper

2
Design Firm, **Cousins Design**
Art Director, **Michael A. Cousins**
Designer, **Mark D. Landry**
Illustrator, **Mark D. Landry**
Copywriter, **Florence D'Emilia**
Client, **Charles D. Gomez, C.P.A.**
Two colors

3
Design Firm, **Nesnadny & Schwartz**
Art Director, **Michael A. Cousins**
Designer, **Mark D. Landry**
Illustrator, **Mark D. Landry**
Copywriter, **Florence D'Emilia**
Client, **Charles D. Gomez, C.P.A.**
Two colors

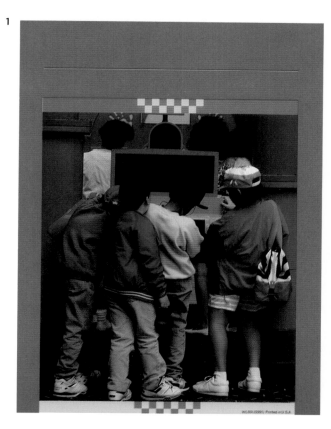

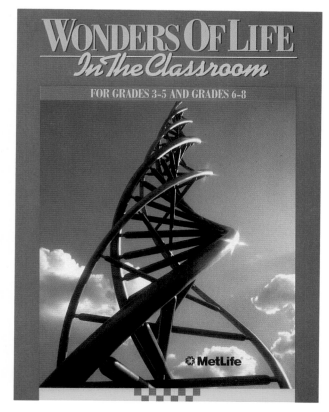

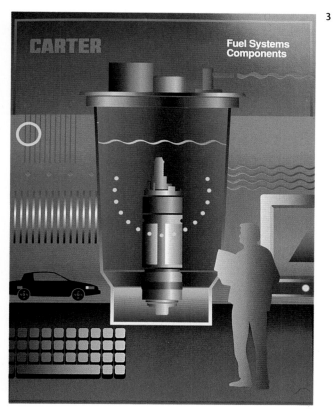

1
Design Firm, **Csoka/Benato/Fleurant, Inc.**
Art Director, **Robert Fleurant**
Designer, **George Benato**
Illustrator, **Werner Kappes**
Photographer, **Ray Buonanno**
Copywriter, **Metropolitan Life Health & Safety Education Division**
Client, **Metropolitan Life Health & Safety Education Division**
Five colors on Consolidated Productolith

2
Design Firm, **Paul Davis Studio**
Art Director, **Paul Davis**
Designer, **Lisa Mazur**
Illustrator, **Paul Davis**
Photographer, **Carol Rosegg/Martha Swope**
Copywriter, **Myrna Davis**
Client, **Stella Adler Conservatory of Acting**
Four colors on Mohawk P/C 100

3
Design Firm, **Pangborn Design, Ltd.**
Art Director, **Dominic Pangborn**
Designer, **Ted Zablocki**
Illustrator, **Han-Eung Kim**
Photographer, **LK Photographic**
Copywriter, **Carter Automotive**
Client, **Carter Automotive**
Four process colors/one PMS color, one gloss varnish on 100-lb. LOE gloss cover

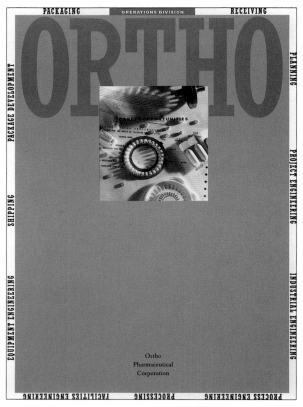

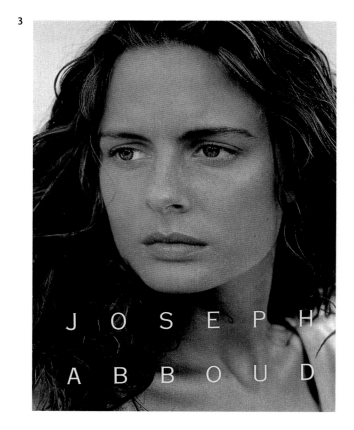

Success has no limits

THE DU PONT MERCK PHARMACEUTICAL COMPANY

1
Design Firm, **Nesnadny & Schwartz**
Art Director, **Joyce Nesnadny/**
Mark Schwartz
Designer, **Joyce Nesnadny**
Photographer, **Tony Festa**
Copywriter, **Ortho**
Pharmaceutical Corp.
Client, **Ortho Pharmaceutical Corp.**
Nine colors on Warren Lustro

2
Design Firm, **Nesnadny & Schwartz**
Art Director, **Joyce Nesnadny/**
Mark Schwartz
Designer, **Joyce Nesnadny**
Photographer, **Tony Festa/**
Mark Schwartz
Copywriter, **Ortho**
Pharmaceutical Corp.
Client, **Ortho Pharmaceutical Corp.**
Nine colors on Warren Lustro

3
Design Firm, **Tyler Smith**
Art Director, **Tyler Smith**
Designer, **Tyler Smith**
Photographer, **Fabrizio Ferri**
Client, **Joseph Abboud**
Five colors on Warren

Fashion photos merged with texture to
create a tactile effect.

4
Design Firm, **DMCD**
Art Director, **Richard Downes**
Designer, **Tom Neilson**
Illustrator, **Holland**
Photographer, **Du Pont/Stock**
Copywriter, **Roger Morris**
Client, **Du Pont Merck**
Six colors on Reflections

1

CORPORATE BANKING SERVICES

Central Banks

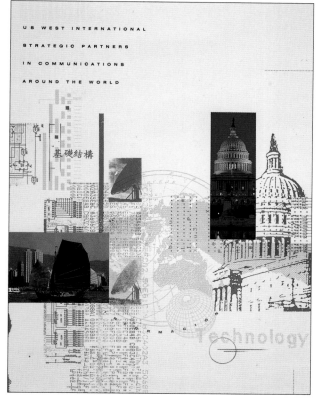

2

US WEST INTERNATIONAL

STRATEGIC PARTNERS

IN COMMUNICATIONS

AROUND THE WORLD

基礎結構

Technology

3

UNITED STATES SAVINGS BONDS

IN TODAY'S PERSPECTIVE

4

The World of Amoco Corporation

AMOCO

1
Design Firm, **Lee Reedy Design Associates, Inc.**
Art Director, **Lee Reedy**
Designer, **Lee Reedy**
Illustrator, **Lee Reedy**
Photographer, **Frank Cruz**
Client, **Central Bank**
Five colors on Centura gloss

2
Design Firm, **Lee Reedy Design Associates, Inc.**
Art Director, **Lee Reedy**
Designer, **Lee Reedy/Heather Bartlett**
Illustrator, **Matthew McFarren**
Client, **U.S. West International**
Five colors on Quintessence dull

3
Design Firm, **Lee Reedy Design Associates, Inc.**
Art Director, **Lee Reedy**
Designer, **Lee Reedy**
Illustrator, **Heidi Krakauer**
Client, **U.S. West Communications**
Three colors on Kromekote, UV Ultra

4
Design Firm, **Clarion Marketing and Communications**
Art Director, **Robert Frankle**
Designer, **Robert Frankle**
Copywriter, **Lauretta Harris**
Client, **Amoco Corp.**
Five colors on Reflections

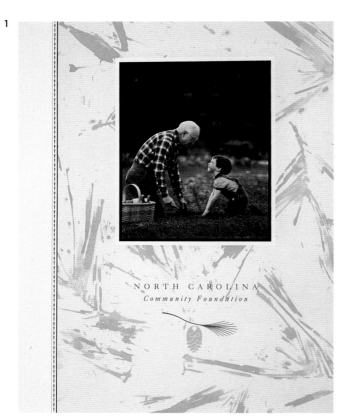

NORTH CAROLINA
Community Foundation

APPIAN

CIVIL AND

MUNICIPAL

ENGINEERS

3

1991 ANNUAL REPORT
NORTH CAROLINA ALTERNATIVE ENERGY CORPORATION

Seeking energy
solutions to make a
world of difference in
North Carolina

ÆC

4

1
Design Firm, **Sally Johns Design**
Creative Director, **Sally Johns**
Designer, **Jeff Dale**
Illustrator, **Jeff Dale**
Photographer, **Steve Murray**
Copywriter, **Debbie Lee**
Client, **North Carolina
Community Foundation**
Four process colors/two PMS colors and
a varnish on Karma cover

2
Design Firm, **Sally Johns Design**
Creative Director, **Sally Johns**
Designer, **Jeff Dale**
Copywriter, **Marvin Johns**
Client, **Appian Consulting Engineers**
Four process colors/one metallic PMS
color and varnish on Vintage gloss cover

3
Design Firm, **Sally Johns Design**
Creative Director, **Sally Johns**
Designer, **Jeff Dale**
Illustrator, **Jeff Dale**
Photographer, **Chip Henderson**
Copywriter, **Mary-Russell Roberson**
Client, **North Carolina Alternative
Energy Corp.**
Four process colors/one PMS color and
varnish on Evergreen matte cover

4
Design Firm, **Communication Arts, Inc.**
Art Director, **Richard Foy**
Designer, T. **Keith Harley**
Photographer, **Michael Barber
Architecture**
Copywriter, **Michael Barber
Architecture**
Client, **Michael Barber Architecture**
Five colors on Quintessence

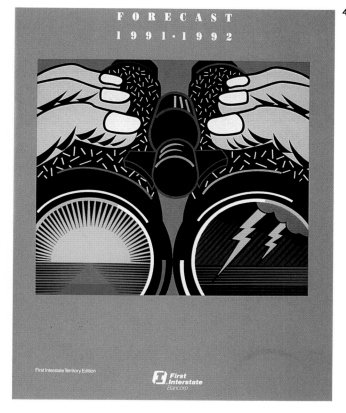

1
Design Firm, **Clarion Marketing
and Communications**
Art Director, **Robert Frankle**
Designer, **Robert Frankle**
Photographer, **Brad Guice**
Copywriter, **Lauretta Harris**
Client, **Amoco Corp.**
Four colors on Ikonofix

2
Design Firm, **Pangborn Design, Ltd.**
Art Director, **Dominic Pangborn**
Designer, **Laura Mysliwiec**
Illustrator, **Laura Mysliwiec/
Peter Schade**
Copywriter, **Children's Hospital
of Michigan**
Client, **Children's Hospital of Michigan**
Four process colors/one PMS color on
Warren Lustro gloss

3
Design Firm, **Shimokochi/
Reeves Design**
Art Director, **Mamoru Shimokochi/
Anne Reeves**
Designer, **Mamoru Shimokochi/
Anne Reeves**
Illustrator, **Mamoru Shimokochi**
Client, **First Interstate Bank**
Eight colors

4
Design Firm, **Shimokochi/
Reeves Design**
Art Director, **Mamoru Shimokochi/
Anne Reeves**
Designer, **Mamoru Shimokochi/
Anne Reeves**
Illustrator, **Mamoru Shimokochi**
Client, **First Interstate Bank**
Six colors

*The illustration for this piece was created
using Adobe Illustrator.*

A COOL $100 COULD BE YOURS DURING OUR SUMMER LOAN SALE

1
Design Firm, **Adele Bass & Co. Design**
Art Director, **Adele Bass**
Designer, **Adele Bass**
Photographer, **Rob Outwater**
Copywriter, **Sharynn Bass**
Client, **Los Angeles Federal Credit Union**
Four process colors on 80-lb. Brilliant Art
gloss cover

*The $100 bill image inside the ice cube is
computer-simulated.*

2
Design Firm, **Adele Bass & Co. Design**
Art Director, **Adele Bass**
Designer, **Adele Bass**
Illustrator, **Adele Bass**
Client, **Rancho Federal Credit Union**
Six colors on 80-lb. Lustro dull cream

1
Design Firm, **Lee Reedy Design Associates, Inc.**
Art Director, **Lee Reedy**
Designer, **Lee Reedy**
Illustrator, **Lee Reedy**
Copywriter, **Nancy McCarthy**
Client, **The Potato Board**
Two colors on Speckletone

1

1
Design Firm, **George Tscherny, Inc.**
Art Director, **George Tscherny**
Designer, **George Tscherny/Elizabeth Laub**
Copywriter, **Kim Kassab**
Client, **SEI Corp.**
Three colors

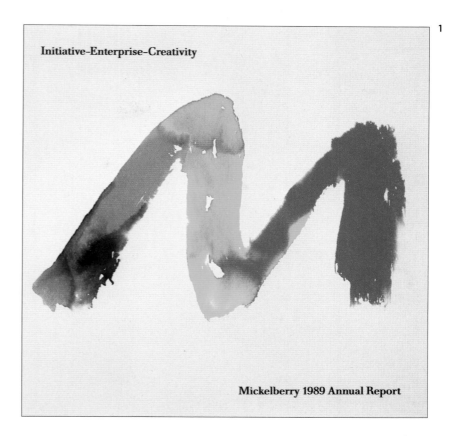

Initiative-Enterprise-Creativity

Mickelberry 1989 Annual Report

SEi '89

1
Design Firm, **George Tscherny, Inc.**
Art Director, **George Tscherny**
Designer, **George Tscherny**
Illustrator, **George Tscherny**
Photographer, **Bill Hayward**
Client, **Mickelberry Corp.**
Eight colors on Mohawk Navajo

2
Design Firm, **George Tscherny, Inc.**
Art Director, **George Tscherny**
Designer, **George Tscherny/Elizabeth Laub**
Copywriter, **Kathleen Wicker**
Client, **SEI Corp.**
Six colors on Strathmore Writing cover

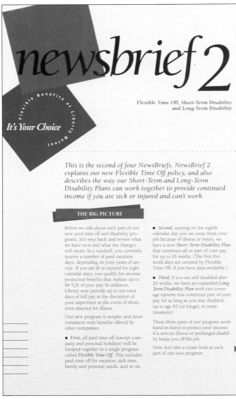

1
Design Firm, **Portfolio**
Art Director, **Wendy Terry**
Designer, **Wendy Terry/Busha Husak/Sally**
Stevens/Carmen Weltner
Copywriter, **Hewitt**
Client, **Liberty Mutual**
Five colors on 80-lb. Glen Eagle dull cover

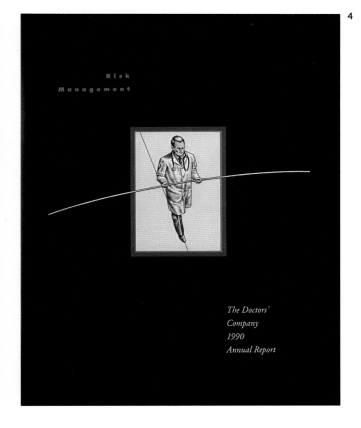

1
Design Firm, **Hornall Anderson Design Works**
Art Director, **Jani Drewfs**
Designer, **Jani Drewfs/Paula Cox/ Denise Weir**
Photographer, **Kevin Latona (cover)**
Copywriter, **Mark Phillips**
Client, **Plum Creek Timber Co.**
Six colors on Quintessence dull

2
Design Firm, **Akagi Design**
Art Director, **Doug Akagi**
Designer, **Doug Akagi/Sharrie Brooks/ Lenore Bartz**
Photographer, **Paul Margolies**
Client, **U.S. Windpower**

3
Design Firm, **Chermayeff & Geismar, Inc.**
Art Director, **Ivan Chermayeff**
Photographer, **Chris Maynard/ Jon Love/Richard Barnes/ Gamma One Conversions**
Copywriter, **Scripps Howard**
Client, **Scripps Howard**
Four process colors

4
Design Firm, **Colonna, Farrell: Design Associates**
Art Director, **Cynthia Maguire**
Designer, **Cynthia Maguire**
Illustrator, **Ed Lindloff**
Photographer, **Will Mosgrove**
Copywriter, **Robert Urbaner**
Client, **The Doctors' Co.**
Four process colors/two PMS colors on coated recycled stock

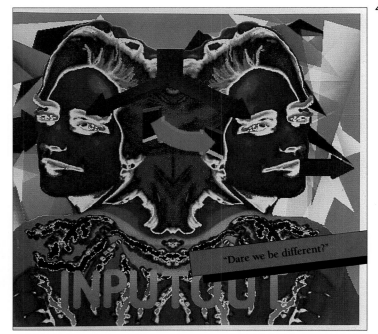

1
Design Firm, **Smith Art Direction
& Design Associates**
Art Director, **James Smith**
Designer, **Sam Gunn/Carol Konkowski**
Illustrator, **Lucille Simonetti**
Copywriter, **Liz MacAvery**
Client, **Bell Atlantic**
Four process colors on 80-lb. Mead
Offset Enamel cover

2
Design Firm, **Held & Diedrich
Design, Inc.**
Art Director, **Douglas D. Diedrich/
Tim Gant**
Designer, **Douglas D. Diedrich/
Tim Gant**
Illustrator, **Tim Gant**
Photographer, **Michael J. Roccaforte**
Copywriter, **Mary Dugger**
Client, **The Phoenix Theatre**
Four colors on Productolith

3
Design Firm, **Glenn Martinez &
Associates**
Art Director, **Kathleen Nelson**
Designer, **Glenn Martinez**
Illustrator, **David Shantz**
Copywriter, **Michelle Hunter**
Client, **The Meritage Association**
Two colors on 63-lb. Monza gloss cover

4
Design Firm, **ACA College of Design**
Art Director, **Marion Allman**
Designer, **Marion Allman**
Copywriter, **Marion Allman**
Client, **ACA College of Design**
Four process colors on 80-lb. Centura
gloss cover

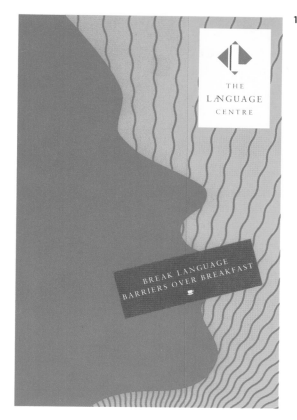

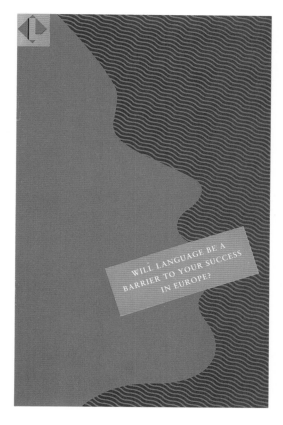

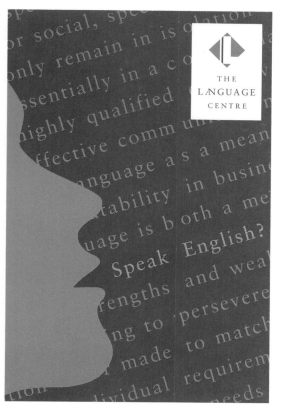

1
Design Firm, **Elmwood**
Art Director, **Clare Marsh**
Designer, **Clare Marsh**
Illustrator, **Clare Marsh**
Photographer, **Bob Walker**
Copywriter, **Nick Hynes**
Client, **Leeds Polytechnic**
Three colors on Skyesilk Ivory

1
Design Firm, **Adele Bass & Co. Design**
Art Director, **Adele Bass**
Designer, **Adele Bass**
Photographer, **Rob Outwater**
Copywriter, **Sharynn Bass**
Client, **Rockwell Federal Credit Union**
Four process colors and spot varnish

2
Design Firm, **Sabin Design**
Art Director, **Marilee Barkert**
Designer, **Tracy Sabin**
Illustrator, **Tracy Sabin**
Copywriter, **Marilee Barkert**
Client, **Fashion Valley**
Four process colors on Quintessence

The windows in this brochure actually open.

3
Design Firm, **Sabin Design**
Art Director, **Marilee Barkert**
Designer, **Tracy Sabin**
Illustrator, **Tracy Sabin**
Copywriter, **Marilee Barkert**
Client, **Fashion Valley**
Four process colors on 70-lb. Speckletone text

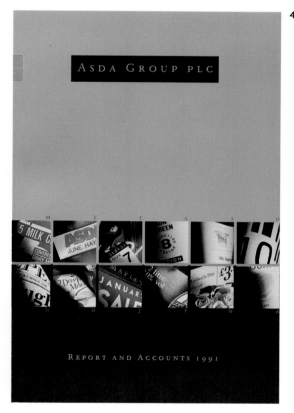

1
Design Firm, **Wilder-Fearn**
and Associates
Art Director, **Gary Fearn**
Designer, **Bill Sontag**
Illustrator, **John Maggerd**
Photographer, **Ron Forth**
Copywriter, **Linda Kaelon**
Client, **The Andrew Jergens Co.**
Five colors and varnish on Warren Lustro

2
Design Firm, **Notovitz Design, Inc.**
Art Director, **Joseph Notovitz/Gil Livne**
Designer, **Gil Livne**
Photographer, **Baker Vale**
Copywriter, **Joseph Notovitz**
Client, **Time**
Five colors on Vintage

3
Design Firm, **Nesnadny & Schwartz**
Art Director, **Okey Nestor/**
Mark Schwartz
Designer, **Okey Nestor**
Client, **Ohio Permanente**
Nine colors on Quintessence

4
Design Firm, **Elmwood**
Art Director, **Clare Marsh**
Designer, **Clare Marsh**
Photographer, **Doug Currie/**
Sue Hiscoe/Bob Walker
Client, **ASDA Group Plc.**
Six colors and varnish on Ikonorex
Special matte, White and Ivory

INDEX

DIRECTORY

ACA College Of Design
2528 Kemper Lane
Cincinnati, OH 45206

Adele Bass and Co. Design
758 East Colorado Blvd.
#209
Pasadena, CA 91101-2129

Akagi Design
632 Commercial Street
San Francisco, CA 94111-2504

Alan Chan Design Co.
201-3, 2F Shiu Lam Bldg.
23 Luard Road
Wanchai,
HONG KONG

Allen Moore & Associates
132 West 21st Street
12th Floor
New York, NY 10011

Art Chantry Design
PO Box 4069
Seattle, WA 98121

Ascent Communications
724 West Lewis Street
Livingston, MT 59047

Bernhardt/Fudyma Design Group
133 East 36th Street
New York, NY 10016

Besser Joseph Partners
1546 7th Street #301
Santa Monica, CA 90401

Bradford Lawton Design Group
719 Avenue E
San Antonio, TX 78215

Butler Kosh Brooks
1355 N. Coronado Street
Los Angeles, CA 90026

Carbone Smolan Associates
22 West 19th Street
New York, NY 10011

Charles S. Anderson Design Co.
30 N. First
Minneapolis, MN 55401

Chermayeff & Geismar Associates
15 East 26th Street
12th Floor
New York, NY 10010

Clarion Marketing + Communication
340 Pemberwick Road
Greenwich, CT 06927

Clifford Selbert Design
2067 Massachusetts Avenue
3rd Floor
Cambridge, MA 02140

Colonna, Farrell:Design
1335 Main Street
St. Helena, CA 94574

Cordella Design, Inc.
725 Boylston Street
Boston, MA 02116

Communication Arts Inc.
1112 Pearl Street
Boulder, CO 80302

Cousins Design
599 Broadway
New York, NY 10012

Creative Company
3276 Commercial St. SE
Salem, OR 97302

Csoka/Benato/Fleurant Inc.
134 W. 26th Street
New York, NY 10001

DMCD
911 Washington Street
Wilmington, DE 19801

Davies Associates
5817 Uplander Way
Culver City, CA 90230

Dennard Creative, Inc.
13601 Preston Road
Dallas, TX 75240

Design North, Inc.
8007 Douglas Avenue
Racine, WI 53402

Donovan and Green
One Madison Avenue
New York, NY 10010

Elmwood Design, Ltd.
Elmwood House, Ghyll Guiseley
Leeds, West Yorkshire
LS20 9LT England

Emery/Poe Design
330 Ritch Street
San Francisco, CA 94107

Frankfurt Gips Balkind
244 East 58th Street
New York, NY 10022

George Tscherny, Inc.
238 East 72nd Street
New York, NY 10021

Glenn Martinez & Associates
15 Third Street
Santa Rosa, CA 95401

Graphic Partners
Gladstone Court
179 Canongate
Edinburgh, EH8 8BN
SCOTLAND

Gray Baumgarten Layport
2275 Swallow Hill Road
Pittsburgh, PA 15228

Hafeman Design Group
935 W. Chestnut
Suite 203
Chicago, IL 60622

Handler Group Inc.
55 West 45th Street
New York, NY 10036

Held & Diedrich Design Inc.
703 East 30th Street #16
Indianapolis, IN 46205

Herbst Lazar Bell Inc.
345 N. Canal Street
Chicago, IL 60606

Hill Holiday Design
200 Clarendon Street
Boston, MA 02116

Hornall Anderson Design Works
1008 Western Avenue
Floor 6
Seattle, WA 98104

Images
1835 Hampden Ct
Louisville, KY 40205

Integrate, Inc.
503 South High Street
Columbus, OH 43215

Jack Tom Design
80 Varick Street
Suite 3B
New York, NY 10013

Jamie Davison Design, Inc.
2325 Third Street
Suite 339
San Francisco, CA 94107

Knut Hartmann Design
Corneliusstrasse 8
6000 Frankfurt
GERMANY

Knoth & Meads
401 West A Street
Suite 1100
San Diego, CA 92101-7905

Kollberg/Johnson Assoc. Inc.
7 West 18th Street
New York, NY 10011

Lee Reedy Design Associates
1542 Williams Street
Denver, CO 80218

Marsha Drebelbis Studio
8150 Brookriver Drive
Suite 208-S
Dallas, TX 75247

Martin Ross Design
1125 Xerxes Avenue So.
Minneapolis, MN 55405

McCargar Design
3906 Silverado Trail
Calistoga, CA 94515-9611

Michael Stanard Inc.
1000 Main Street
Evanston, IL 60202

Morla Design
463 Bryant Street
San Francisco, CA 94107

Morris/Beecher Inc.
1000 Potomac Street NW
Terrace
Washington, DC 20007-3501

Muller + Co.
112 West Nine
Kansas City, MO 64105

Myklebust Brockman Graphics
3628 East Avenue South
LaCrosse, WI 54601

Nesnadny & Schwartz
10803 Magnolia Drive
Cleveland, OH 44106

Notovitz Design Inc.
47 East 19th Street
New York, NY 10003

O & J Design, Inc.
9 West 29th Street
New York, NY 10001

Pangborn Design, Ltd.
275 Iron Street
Detroit, MI 48207

Pat Gorman/Manhattan Design
47 West 13th Street
New York, NY 10011

Patterson Wood
133 West 19th Street
New York, NY 10011

Paul Davis Studio
14 East 4th Street
New York, NY 10012

Pinkhaus Design Corp.
2424 South Dixie Highway
Suite 201
Miami, FL 33133

Platinum Design Inc.
14 West 23rd Street
New York, NY 10010

Porter/Matjasich & Associates
154 West Hubbard
Suite 504
Chicago, IL 60610

Portfolio
38 Newbury Street
Boston, MA 02116

RGF&L
100 Metro Park South
Laurence, NJ 08857-3221

Raymond Bennett Design Assoc. Ltd.
3/345 Pacific Hwy
Crows Nest NSW,
AUSTRALIA 2065

Richard Danne & Associates
126 Fifth Avenue
New York, NY 10011

Richardson or Richardson
1301 East Bethany Home
Phoenix, AZ 85014

Rick Eiber Design
4649 Sunnyside North
#242
Seattle, WA 98103

Rowley Associates, Inc.
12739 E. Doubletree Ranch Road
Scottsdale, AZ 85259

SHR Design Communications
8700 East Via De Ventura
Scottsdale, AZ 85258

Sabin Design
13476 Ridley Road
San Diego, CA 92129

Sackett Design Associates
864 Fulsom Street
San Francisco, CA 94107-1123

Sally Johns Design Studio
1040 Washington Street
P.O. Box 10833
Raleigh, NC 27605

Samenwerkende Ontwerpers
Herengracht 160
1016 BN
Amsterdam,
THE NETHERLANDS

Sayles Graphic Design
308 Eighth Street
Des Moines, IA 50309

Shannon Design Associates
355 Settlers Road
Holland, MI 49423

Shimokochi/Reeves Design
4465 Wilshire Blvd.
#100
Los Angeles, CA 90010

Smith Art Direction and Design Assoc.
205 Thomas Street
Glen Ridge, NJ 07028

Sommese Design
481 Glenn Road
State College, PA 16803

Steve Galit & Associates
5105 Monroe Road
Charlotte, NC 28205

Steve Lundgren Graphic Design
6524 Walker Street
Suite 205
Minneapolis, MN 55426

Stillman Design Associates
17 East 89th Street
New York, NY 10128

Stylism
307 East 6th Street 4B
New York, NY 10003

Taylor & Ives, Inc.
1001 6th Ave
New York, NY 10018

Taylor/Christian Advertising
8035 Broadway
San Antonio, TX 78209

Tharp Did It
50 University Avenue
Suite 21
Los Gatos, CA 95030

The Kuester Group
81 South Ninth Street
Suite 300
Minneapolis, MN 55402

The Weller Institute for Cure of Design
PO Box 726
3091 W. Fawn Drive
Park City, UT 84060-0726

Tyler Smith Design
127 Dorrance Street
Providence, RI 02903

Vardimon Design
87 Shlomo Hamelech Street
Tel Aviv 64512
ISRAEL

WRK
602 Westport Road
Kansas City, MO 64111

Walcott-Ayers & Shore
1230 Preservation Pk Way
Oakland, CA 94612

Walter McCord Graphic Design
2014 Cherokee Parkway
Louisville, KY 40204

Wiggin Design, Inc.
23 Old Kings Hwy.
Darien, CT 06820

Wilder-Fearn & Associates, Inc.
644 Linn Street
Suite 416
Cincinnati, OH 45203